FIVE P'S TO A

WOW!

BUSINESS

FIVE P'S TO A

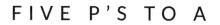

WOW!

BUSINESS

AN EASY-TO-UNDERSTAND, EASY-TO-IMPLEMENT, PRACTICAL GUIDE TO BUSINESS SUCCESS

BILL MATTHEWS

SOUND WISDOM
P.O. Box 310
Shippensburg, PA 17257-0310

For more information on publishing and distribution rights, call 717-530-2122 or *info@ soundwisdom.com*.

Quantity Sales. Special discounts are available on quantity purchases by corporations, associations, and others. For details, contact the Sales Department at Sound Wisdom.

While efforts have been made to verify information contained in this publication, neither the author nor the publisher assumes any responsibility for errors, inaccuracies, or omissions.

While this publication is chock-full of useful, practical information, it is not intended to be legal or accounting advice. All readers are advised to seek competent lawyers and accountants to follow laws and regulations that may apply to specific situations.

The reader of this publication assumes responsibility for the use of the information. The author and publisher assume no responsibility or liability whatsoever on the behalf of the reader of this publication.

ISBN 13 TP: 978-1-64095-035-1
ISBN 13 Ebook: 978-1-64095-036-8

Previously published in 2012 under ISBN 978-1-57074-041-1

For Worldwide Distribution, Printed in the U.S.A.
1 2 3 4 5 6 7 8 / 21 20 19 18

Cover/Jacket designer Eileen Rockwell

Thank you……..

*to my wife, Janet, and my entire family
for your continued encouragement,*

*and to the hundreds of business owners
who have placed their trust in me.*

Table of Contents

CHAPTER 1

"Ouch," "Ho-Hum," "Gee-Whiz," and **"WOW!"**

"Ouch," "Ho-Hum," "Gee-Whiz," and **"WOW!"**

Before we begin, you might be asking yourself, "Who is this 'Bill Matthews' guy, and what qualifies him to be giving advice about running an effective business?" Like many other baby-boomers, I chose the path of getting as much education as I could stand, with the hope that a "Fortune 500" company would sweep me off my feet and provide me with an exciting career until I retired with my gold watch. So that's exactly what I did. After navigating my way to the executive level I had hoped to reach someday, I realized that I had achieved my goal and still had about twenty-five more years to work! It was time for a change, so I left the comfortable "Fortune 500" environment to run a privately-held company where things moved much faster. It was an eye-opening experience to say the least, including some very painful lessons along the way! We were fortunate to have successfully grown the business, eventually attracting the attention of a publicly-held company that offered to acquire us.

After selling the company, some of my friends who owned businesses began to ask me for input on a variety of issues facing their organizations. I quickly realized how passionate I was about sharing my experiences, including the mistakes I had made along the way, so I decided my next career would be as a business consultant. To date I have had at least some level of involvement with nearly a thousand organizations, and have worked very closely with a few hundred of them. It's been an incredible experience that continues to get me pumped-up with every new engagement. These are wonderful human beings who are the backbone of our economy, and are creating jobs in our communities.

A few years ago I felt compelled to write about some of the most common factors that cause problems for business owners. The book was entitled *Don't Step in the Entremanure*, and was presented as my answer to the question, "How do businesses get in trouble?" Now I feel it's time to write a book that takes an optimistic perspective by identifying the factors that make businesses **successful**, so hopefully what follows will be of help to those who read it.

Even though I've had the opportunity to work closely with such a large number of businesses, I've encountered an extremely small percentage that I would categorize as having reached what I call "WOW!" status.

To me, "WOW!" means a business is impeccably managed in every aspect. In other words, no matter how closely I scrutinize their daily practices, I can't find any area of their business where they need help. Or, if something isn't exactly what it should be, the business owner is already aware of it and is taking the necessary steps to correct it. That's my definition of a "WOW!" business, and why they're few and far between.

It's important to stress that none of them started that way. In fact, they worked diligently for many years to reach the point when I could utter "WOW!" to myself when examining them closely. It required them to make significant changes and tough decisions to move themselves into the "WOW!" category.

Before outlining exactly what needs to be done to become a "WOW!" organization, it's important to understand why there aren't more of them, and how businesses end up falling short. Over the years I've classified businesses into four general categories:

1. *"Ouch"*

2. *"Ho-Hum"*

3. *"Gee-Whiz"*

4. *"WOW!"*

Organizations in the "Ouch" category are those where the leaders have lost control of their businesses, as well as their personal lives. Those in the "Ho-Hum" stage are doing well enough to keep the owner satisfied, but are likely very vulnerable to regressing back into the "Ouch" category if they don't pay attention to the changes going on around them. "Gee-Whiz" businesses are generally very well-managed and doing a lot of things right, often referred to as "leaders in the market," and less likely to ever regress all the way back into "Ouch" territory, even though they may periodically find themselves at least temporarily in the "Ho-Hum" stage. A precise description of those in the "WOW!" category will be the focus of the remaining chapters of this book. For now, let's examine "Ouch," "Ho-Hum," and "Gee-Whiz."

The Downward Spiral to "Ouch"

Regardless of whether you started the business yourself, purchased it from someone else, or followed in the footsteps of a family member who used to lead the organization, you might recall how excited you were to be running your own enterprise and taking control of your life. You were tired of working for someone else and wanted to pursue the "American Dream" of owning your own business. You probably had a specific skill set that was acquired on the job or learned in the classroom. In some cases it may have been a combination of both. Typical examples are software development, plumbing, accounting, engineering, heating/air conditioning technician, etc...

You took that technical skill, went "out on your own," and began to deliver your services to those who truly valued your talents. You probably also had a strong work ethic, honesty, integrity, and a pleasant personality that endeared your customers to you. Perhaps most importantly you had a true PASSION for what you were doing.

As you grew, you eventually had to bring-in one or more people to help you deliver your product or service. Your day-to-day role changed from player, to player/coach, where you did some of the work and also supervised others. If you were blessed with strong employees, you may have been able to let them work relatively independently. If your employees were not experienced or reliable, you likely found yourself overseeing them for much of the work day.

As a result of this changing environment, you found that you spent more and more of your day acting as a "manager," yet you had little or no training in the *profession* of management. It's important to note here that being a manager is actually a profession, just like being an engineer or plumber. Like any other profession, it requires training. Not only were you not professionally trained to be a "manager," you might not even *like* that role! That's understandable since many business owners would much rather spend their time doing the things they were trained to do, like developing software, versus managing a group of software developers.

As your role moved from player, to player/coach, and then to coach, you began to feel like you were losing control. The employees were requiring far too much of your time, and it was taking a toll on your personal life. Perhaps you were missing more and more of your child's ballgames or recitals, or were observing your employees leaving work at 5:00 while you stayed later to finish their work (some of whom may have been earning more than you!). If you worked in an organization where you shared ownership with a sibling or business partner, your spouse might have been complaining that you work harder than your brother, sister, or partner.

If you were fortunate to have at least one very strong and reliable employee, you may have gifted or sold some stock to that employee, a decision that almost always causes future problems, even if it seems like a great idea at the time.

If you did not start the business yourself, but have led the enterprise for a while, you are likely to have experienced many of the same things mentioned above. This is definitely an "Ouch" situation!

"Ho-Hum"

Assuming you finally reached the point where you could no longer bear to have your personal life and business life out of control, you probably took some major steps to change things. Perhaps you hired people with stronger skill sets, sought the advice of outside experts, terminated one or more people who were holding the company back, stopped doing business with customers who didn't "fit," intentionally reduced the size of the business to simplify things, or made some other key decision(s) to regain control.

As a result of your assertive actions, the business began to do better, and your personal life improved. In fact, much of the pain subsided and you began to find yourself in a new comfort zone. The business was growing at a reasonable rate, employment was stable, customers seemed to be satisfied, and earnings were relatively good. You found yourself falling into the "Ho-Hum" stage, even though you may not have realized it. After all, what could go wrong?

When you reach this stage, you should be pushing yourself and your employees to take the necessary steps to propel you to the "Gee-Whiz" stage. If not, you could easily be blind-sided and find your business back in the "Ouch" category. This can be brought about by such things as a new competitor entering the market, an existing competitor introducing a new product or technology, a major quality problem, loss of a key employee, or countless other events that you might have been able to anticipate or avoid if you hadn't been lulled to sleep in the "Ho-Hum" stage.

"Gee-Whiz"

If you were perceptive enough to realize you were stuck in the "Ho-Hum" stage, and were willing to do whatever necessary to advance to the "Gee-Whiz" category, you probably recognized the need to make additional advances in the skill sets of your people. I'm absolutely convinced that **the biggest single reason why business owners advance to the "Gee-Whiz" category is that they are willing to invest in employees who have the skills required to take them to the next level.** This is not easy to do. Indeed, many key employees may have been with the company from the start—how do you part ways with long-term employees who might also be close friends, or even relatives? In many cases, the solution is not to replace them, but to bring in a highly qualified outsider between the owner and the long-time employee(s). Occasionally, it can actually be the **business owner's** limited competency and skills that present the major obstacle to growth.

In addition to making the necessary changes in personnel, when you entered the "Gee-Whiz" category you committed more time to strategic thinking/planning, put additional controls in place to make sure your business stayed on track and that employees were accountable, and began to seek advice from an outside board consisting of people who had skill sets that your business needed, but couldn't afford to hire as employees.

It will probably come as no surprise that "Gee-Whiz" companies with strong skill sets, a plan, and an outside board, are much less likely to regress back to the "Ho-Hum" stage because the leader is being continuously challenged to think about things outside of the day-to-day operational activities that could otherwise consume attention.

Some Troubling Symptoms

Later in this book we'll provide a much more detailed tool for analyzing the stage of your current business. For now, though, here are some typical comments from business owners who bounce back and forth between "Ouch" and "Ho-Hum:"

"There just aren't enough hours in the day. I've lost control of my time."

"I had a lot more fun when I didn't have any employees."

"I'm not earning enough for the hours and effort I'm expending."

"I don't have anyone to talk to about my issues. My spouse is tired of hearing me complain."

"I know I need more talented people in my business, but I can't afford them."

"I'm afraid of losing everything."

"My business partner/brother/sister/friend isn't pulling his or her weight in the business."

"My personal life is a mess because of the business."

"My employees just aren't being held accountable."

"It seems like I have to do things that others in my business are supposed to be doing."

"Regardless of whether we make money or lose it, I have no idea why! That scares me."

"How can my income statement show that I had a profitable month, but I'm out of cash?"

The statements above are not the real problems, but only *symptoms* of problems that can be corrected through an effective, on-going system of professional management.

The traditional American medical model is a great example of how we can begin to address the obstacles that often hold us back. As patients, we typically seek medical help by describing some sort of annoying or painful symptom, and rely on a medical professional to diagnose the cause and prescribe both a temporary, and permanent, solution. For example, consider the person who plays a lot of tennis, develops chronic elbow pain, and seeks the help of his/her family doctor, known better today as the "primary care physician." After weighing the treatment options, the physician offers the following advice: "I can inject the joint with cortisone, but I would recommend some preventive measures to reduce the likelihood of this occurring again." In essence, the physician is telling the patient that cortisone is a temporary solution, and the inflammation could occur again if certain pro-active steps are not taken to prevent it.

Many business owners engage consultants to help in a specific area. For example, if they are not happy with their selling efforts, they might bring-in a specialist to help them identify their ideal prospects, create cost-effective ways to market to those prospects, hire and train the right sales people, and develop formal sales processes, procedures, budgets, quotas, and controls. All too often, after the consultant leaves, things gradually revert back to the way they were. Why? Leadership in the organization is not strong enough to sustain the discipline and accountability that had been established with the consultant's help.

Rather than simply treating the symptoms, the real answer is to adopt a comprehensive professional management "system" by which you effectively and successfully run your organization day-in and day-out. An organization that is truly professionally managed has "built-in" checks and balances that enable it to remain stable, even in the most unstable business environments. There are many books and articles written about professional management systems, some more academic than others, but the common thread is that it must be a "system" if it is to be effective in maintaining control and balance.

Unfortunately, most businesses are not in the pro-active mode of a professional management system, but prefer to get "quick fix" after "quick fix" in order to survive, much like the temporary relief of a cortisone injection. At first it might be difficult to understand why any organization would not want to adopt a pro-active professional management system, but the reason is more obvious than you might think. It takes a lot of work and change for an organization to become truly professionally managed, and too few business owners have the desire or courage to make those changes happen.

In the next chapter, we'll begin to outline exactly how to move out of "Ouch," "Ho-Hum," and "Gee-Whiz," and transform an organization to the "WOW!" category.

CHAPTER 2

It's All About the
"Five P's!"

It's All About the "Five P's!"

Before going any further, it's important to note that perhaps 20 to 30 percent of the companies I've worked with could be classified as well-managed, "Gee-Whiz" organizations, even though only a small percentage of them advance to what I would call "WOW!" companies. In examining what those "WOW!" organizations have in common, I must admit that it was a real eye-opener for me. Overall, there are five key factors that all of them share. It is strictly coincidental that those five factors all start with the letter "P," but since it worked out that way, here are **"The Five P's:"**

1. PLANNING as a Perpetual Process

The first key ingredient is **PLANNING**, not as a one-time or periodic event, but a **perpetual process**. In other words, they run their businesses using planning as an integral part of what they do every single day without exception. For them, planning is a process, NOT a project. They have a clear Vision, continuously evaluate the changing external environment in which they operate, leverage and invest in their key strengths (the things that differentiate them from their competitors), overcome their weaknesses, and continue to refocus on the issues and opportunities that must be addressed to achieve the Vision. While they might go off-site annually to take a fresh look at the plan, many of them probably don't have to do that because they've adopted perpetual planning as a way of life. They also have the necessary business controls (budgets, forecasts, "dashboards," etc...) in place to monitor performance against the plan.

2. PEOPLE Who Fit, Today and Tomorrow

The second ingredient will come as no surprise. Each organization has highly-qualified, purpose-driven **PEOPLE** who have the right attitude that makes them a "fit" for the culture. They have created an organizational structure (chart) that is determined by their plan, and then filled those "boxes" with employees who are qualified today, and are likely to remain qualified for at least a few additional years as the company continues to grow. That is, these organizations place great emphasis on hiring and developing people who offer both the required skill sets, AND the right attitude. They are pro-active and deliberate when it comes to employee development, and when the strategic plan calls for employee horsepower that they don't already have in place, they do not hesitate to hire or develop the talent they need to implement the perpetual plan.

3. PROCESSES

The third ingredient is less obvious. "WOW!" companies have **PROCESSES** in place that are well-documented, precisely followed, and regularly modified to meet the ever-changing demands of the world around them, both inside and outside the company. It's important to note that even "average" employees can follow well-documented processes. However, as the market changes, and processes gradually become less efficient, "average" employees are less likely to either recognize that current processes are out of date, or to have the skills to make the necessary modifications to those processes. On the other hand, strong employees are more apt to recognize the need for change, and to create more efficient processes to meet the ever-changing needs of markets and customers. Well-documented processes tend to reduce costs of operation, improve quality, shorten delivery time, make people more accountable, and contribute to better bottom-line performance. "WOW!" companies recognize these benefits, and actively invest in improved processes.

4. "PERFORMETRICS"

Ingredient number four is something that I like to call **PERFORMETRICS**, based on the premise that "the things we measure are the things that get done."

Performetrics are not limited to the typical budgets, forecasts, dashboards, and other financial measures, but also include specific performance metrics/expected outcomes tied to the strategic plan, and cascade down the organization so that each employee has individual measures that are directly or indirectly tied to the outcomes established in the strategic plan. While there might also be "group" incentives in place, each company places primary emphasis on rewarding individual performance related to measurable outcomes that are *totally within the control* of each employee. We will spend more time later on this topic, including some tools and examples to help identify those things that an employee can truly control.

5. PASSION to Be the Best

In compiling my initial list of "WOW!" companies, I also noticed one additional factor that set them apart—a genuine and relentless **PASSION** to be the best. Companies do NOT necessarily have to demonstrate passion to reach "WOW!" status, but passionate organizations and business owners seem to get there **faster**, and are **less likely to regress** from the "WOW!" category because they continuously strive to stay on top. Passion is most evidently displayed by the organization's leader. Passion is something that you either have, or you don't have. You can't fake it. Your employees and your customers can "feel" it, and can see it in your day-to-day behavior. It isn't something that can be taught, so it isn't a function of education. Rather, it's sort of a "secret ingredient," much like the sugar cookies my mom used to make. Even after she gave everyone the recipe, we could never duplicate the taste!

About this Book

The remainder of this book will outline a step by step process leading to "WOW!" status. In all there are 23 steps that will ultimately be summarized in an easy to follow recipe that is contained in Chapter 9. If you need assistance with implementation, just refer to the explanation provided under each step in the appropriate chapter.

CHAPTER 3

The First "P"

PLANNING as a Perpetual Process

The First **"P"**

PLANNING as a Perpetual Process

Many businesses have strategic plans, but few run their enterprises with an on-going planning process. Instead, they view planning as a project that is normally done annually when the planning team goes off-site and talks about a lot of things, some strategic, and some operational. They then print it, put it in an attractive binder (since it's often a thick document), and place it on a shelf. In essence, they just "checked it off the list" as a project completed, rarely referring to it again until next year's planning event.

The real difference between the "WOW!" companies I've encountered, versus the majority of others, is that "WOW!" organizations view planning as a living, breathing, ***perpetual process***, not a *project*. While the plan may be a very brief and focused document, it takes no less time to create than the thick document that's sitting on the shelf at another company. It defines specific outcomes and due dates with built-in accountabilities that will ensure its implementation and success, and it is regularly and relentlessly reviewed to make sure that it is still accurate so that changes can be made immediately in response to shifts in the marketplace.

What is the appropriate time horizon for strategic planning? The answer to this question varies based upon the industry. For the majority of privately held businesses, a plan that looks three years forward is sufficient, especially if it truly becomes a *perpetual planning process* that **continuously** looks out thirty-six months, versus only taking a fresh look every twelve months. In businesses like pharmaceuticals the time horizon is likely to be significantly further out, whereas in software development companies it might be shorter due to the often brief product life cycle before the next version of the technology must be released. Regardless of how many years the plan looks forward, it should be reviewed and revised at least annually.

For the remainder of this chapter, we'll focus on the first ten steps, which will explain how to create an initial plan, and how to then turn it into a **perpetual process**. We will be using a fictitious company, WOW Pest Control, throughout the remainder of this chapter to illustrate each step of the process. The completed plan for WOW Pest Control is included at the end of the chapter.

Step 1: Create a Personal Vision

The planning process begins with the owner creating a Personal Vision for his/her own life. It has nothing to do with the business, but everything to do with personal dreams, goals, and timetables. This is truly a very personal and confidential exercise to be completed by the business owner and the people who are most important in his/her life. The purpose of the Personal Vision is to make certain that the Vision for the organization (created later) does not present a conflict with the personal dreams of the owner. Unfortunately, many seemingly successful business owners have told me that their personal lives are a mess, even though the business is thriving by most standards. Somewhere along the way, the demands of their business have pulled them away from the people who mean the most to them in their lives. It's a little ironic, since most business owners start their own companies in order to have *more* control over their personal lives, not *less*!

Therefore, my recommendation to all business owners is to set aside the time to create a Personal Vision with their loved ones, and to revisit that Personal Vision periodically. A Personal Vision isn't a cute one-liner; in fact, most are written in a few paragraphs, since the Personal Vision is not meant to be shared with anyone outside those who are closest to the business owner.

This exercise can be challenging when more than one person owns the business, especially if there is a significant age difference between the owners. For example, the factors and people to be considered in each owner's personal life can be significantly more complex when one owner has children at home and the other is an empty-nester getting closer to retirement age. Nonetheless, it's an exercise that can identify issues that need to be addressed much sooner than they might otherwise have emerged on their own.

There is no right or wrong method for creating a Personal Vision. Nor are there any rules regarding what it should look like or how it should be formatted when completed. It is a very private process that begins with each business owner contemplating a variety of questions about the ideal future state of his or her personal life—an opportunity to dream about what the perfect future would look like.

Depending upon the business owner's age or stage of life, it might be appropriate for some owners to look five years out, and others to look as many as 20 years into the future. In fact, some do both.

Regardless of the timeframe selected, here are some typical questions that are used to help create a Personal Vision:

1. What will be my day-to-day activities at work, even if they are the same as today?

2. What percentage of the business will I own? If the percentage is more or less than my current share, from whom will I acquire those additional shares, or who will be the ideal buyer for the shares I relinquish?

3. Will any of my children or other family members be involved in the business? If so, will they be qualified? If not, what needs to be done to qualify them? Will they have ownership? If so, how much will they own, and how will they have acquired that ownership?

4. How will I handle it if one family member wants to be involved in the business, while others don't? What will I do to treat family members equitably, regardless of whether or not they own shares in the business?

5. How much money will I need to completely retire, recognizing that the amount will vary based upon when I decide to stop working?

6. Will there be a qualified successor in the business, either family or non-family? If so, who will that be?

7. Will I have completely sold the business? If so, when will that have occurred, and how will that impact the answers to #5 and #6, above?

8. What hobbies or interests outside of work will I begin, or continue to pursue?

9. Will I be involved with volunteer-type activities? If so, what will those be?

10. Will I be active in any philanthropic efforts? If so, which one(s)?
11. If I have a true passion in life, what is it, and how/ when will I spend more time in that endeavor?
12. What will be a perfect day for me?
13. Where will I be living? Will I be living in different locations at certain times of the year? If so, where? What will my residence(s) look like, even if I still live where I do today?
14. How far away will I be living from those closest to me?

These are only a few of the many considerations in formulating a Personal Vision. After recording your thoughts, then get together with your spouse/significant other to discuss these things in detail, along with the hopes and dreams that *they* have. If appropriate, you may want to involve other family members after you and your spouse have first completed your discussion.

The outcome of these conversations will typically be a few paragraphs that describe the details of your future together outside the business. Ideally this exercise should be done each year, since changes may have occurred in the personal lives of the business owner, spouse/significant other, or other family members since the last discussion. That's why it's important to commit your Personal Vision to writing.

Sample Personal Vision

Here is a sample Personal Vision. In this case, the business owner chose to look five years out. He then met with his spouse and children to discuss his Personal Vision and revise it slightly based on their input:

"In five years, I will have moved from the day-to-day leader of the company to Chairman, where my role will be the chief strategist for the organization, and architect of the culture. I will spend approximately two days per week on the job, and will have relinquished the leadership role to a non-family President whose job will be to mentor my son until he is deemed ready to become President. We will have established a mechanism for my son to gradually purchase my shares as soon as he is ready to be named President, and will concurrently design a plan so that my two daughters are treated equitably, even though they are not involved in the business."

"I will give up golf so that my wife and I can spend time visiting our three children and six grandchildren."

"We will own a condominium in Austin, Texas, near our two daughters. Both of their families live within a half-hour of our condominium. We will also retain ownership of our current residence in Pennsylvania, which will have been updated."

"My wife and I will spend more time as volunteers at the summer youth program connected to our church. She will have relinquished her job as bookkeeper at our company and begin teaching English to adults in our community through an outreach program, while I will serve as a SCORE volunteer one day each week assisting start-up businesses."

"A perfect day would involve waking up to the warm sun, having breakfast with my wife over-looking the forest behind our house, or the lake behind our condominium. We would then ride our bikes for an hour, have lunch together, enjoy our pontoon boat, touch base with our children and grandchildren in person, by phone, or by video-conferencing, get a wonderful "thank you" note from someone who attended the youth camp or received help at SCORE, go out to dinner, and watch the sunset."

Eric owns WOW Pest Control. He and his wife, Stacy, have used the previous list of questions to go through the Personal Vision process, including multiple discussions between one another, as well as their two children, John and Katie. John is nineteen, attends art school, and is likely to never have an interest in any aspect of the business. Katie is twenty-two and will graduate next year with a degree in accounting.

After completion of the family discussions, Eric and Stacy have decided that they will commit at least five more years to aggressively grow the business, even though there may be opportunities along the way to sell it to a large competitor who has twice expressed an interest in acquiring WOW Pest Control. In five years, Eric and Stacy expect to have a better idea regarding Katie's possible interest in joining the family business someday. Both Eric's parents and Stacy's parents are alive and in reasonably good health, but Stacy's parents live about 800 miles from Eric and Stacy. There is, of course, the possibility that the failing health of a parent could cause a change in plans, especially since neither Eric nor Stacy have any siblings who can lend a hand in caring for an ailing parent. Looking further down the road, both Eric and Stacy have also identified their desire to buy a house on the lake that is located very near Stacy's parents as a retreat for themselves and their children, using it only occasionally at first, but more often as they grow older.

At the end of the Personal Vision exercise, they both realized how important it was that they had thoroughly discussed countless scenarios, many of which they had not previously considered. As a result, they saved all of their notes from the discussions and made plans to go through the exercise every January to make absolutely certain that the Vision for their personal lives was up-to-date so it could be the basis of re-evaluating the Vision for WOW Pest Control.

In the sample plan for WOW Pest Control at the end of this chapter, you'll note that the Personal Vision is NOT included as part of the strategic plan. There are two very good reasons why the Personal Vision of the owner is kept confidential. First, it will come as no surprise that it is very private information and few, if any, business owners want to share it. The second reason is less obvious, but extremely important. If Eric and Stacy had decided that they wanted to sell the business in the next two years, that's certainly not something they would want employees to know. Yet it would be a major consideration when re-evaluating their Vision for the company.

Step 2: Establish the Organizational Vision, Mission, Values and Beliefs

(See Sample Plan at the End of This Chapter)

Assuming you are now very comfortable with what you would like to achieve in your own personal life, including a rough timetable, it's time to create a Vision for your organization. Please note that, even after you have created the Vision for your organization, it can still change in the future. In fact, you'll see later in this chapter that you will be objectively evaluating the external environment (the economy, competition, technology, etc...) as you go through the planning process. During that exercise, it is sometimes necessary to modify the Vision for your organization, especially if you find there are environmental factors at work which will make your Vision too simple or difficult to achieve. So please keep this in mind as you create the Organizational Vision.

There are two very important things to remember about an Organizational Vision. First, it should be created by the owner(s), not by a team of people, since it must take into consideration the Personal Vision of each owner. Second, while the Vision statement is often shared with customers and the public at large, it is actually meant for internal use, and is *designed to drive the behavior of your employees every day by providing them with a crystal-clear explanation of exactly where you want to go.*

Organizational Visions are usually written in the future tense, as what you want "to be" or "to become." In the sample plan contained at the end of this chapter, you will note the following Vision: "WOW Pest Control will be the first choice for residential pest control services in Miller County." Ideally, you must be able to actually determine when you've achieved your Vision, so be sure that it can somehow be measured, even if only by a periodic survey of customers. In the case of WOW Pest Control, "first choice" means that homeowners in Miller County would want to contact WOW before any of their competitors due to WOW's impeccable reputation, even if WOW doesn't ultimately get selected. WOW Pest Control has made firm plans to conduct a market survey every two years to measure progress toward their Vision.

Creating the Vision for your organization can be complicated, and you might need help from someone, but it's well worth the effort to achieve total clarity so that your employees know why they come to work every day! It needs to be communicated to your employees over, and over, and over again.

The process of linking your Vision to your plan is much like choosing a destination for your family vacation. You identify a VERY SPECIFIC END POINT (Vision) before you begin. Perhaps it's a beach house at a specific address. You then chart a detailed route that will get you there, (similar to the strategic plan you create to achieve your Vision), and you clearly articulate the end point and the route so that all of your family members are well-informed. In business, and in driving your family to their vacation spot, you don't want people continuously asking, "Where are we going?" or, "Are we almost there?" If you use your GPS system to help you reach your vacation destination, it will remind you of each turn along the way, and might even alert you to detours so you can continue toward your destination despite obstacles that may have arisen. At any point along the way, your GPS system can help you determine your progress toward your destination. Similarly, you'll need controls in place to monitor the progress you make toward your organization's Vision.

Please note that Vision and Mission are often confused with one another. Mission statements are typically written in the present tense. They describe what your organization does, and for whom. For example, "we provide (blank) for (blank)." As you will see in the sample strategic plan at the end of this chapter, WOW Pest Control's Mission is: "WOW Pest Control provides comprehensive, high-quality, environmentally-safe pest control services to homeowners in Miller County."

Values and Beliefs for an organization vary widely, and take many forms. Some prefer to create a Credo or a Pledge. They can be very personal and are often conveyed with significant passion. The key point to remember here is that an organization should never communicate a value, belief, credo, or pledge that stretches the truth. If your organization is not able to actually demonstrate these things by consistent behaviors, then do not list them. That is, resist the urge to list things that you think will "sound good," or that you *hope* to achieve someday. In the WOW Pest Control plan at the end of this chapter, note that they are particularly focused on Values and Beliefs that are consistent with their Mission and Vision.

An Important Consideration Before Steps 3 and 4

Many smaller organizations participate in only one segment. This is precisely the way that WOW Pest Control operates, with all of its efforts focused on residential pest control in Miller County. In that situation, there is only one market segment. As we will see shortly, during the WOW Pest Control planning process, members of the planning team identified three other opportunities worth considering. In each of those three potential market segments there are some very unique differences. For example, if WOW Pest Control decided to provide their services to both homeowners AND businesses, there would be different competitors, and perhaps the strengths WOW has in the residential market would mean nothing when selling to businesses. WOW might have 20 percent market share in the residential market segment, but only be capable of capturing 1 percent in the commercial segment. Indeed, their strategies would be significantly different in those two segments, the action items to support those strategies would vary widely, and the organizational structure/people skills would differ as well.

Thus, before you begin it is crucial to evaluate the external environment (as outlined in the next step) and the SWOT analysis (covered in the step after that) to **make absolutely certain that you have appropriately identified the specific segments in which your business operates/competes.**

One of the most eye-opening exercises in strategic planning is the identification of the ideal attributes of a market segment (group of customers/potential customers). It's a method of determining what makes one alternative better than another. The same tool can also be used to rank the customers you already have, or evaluate the relative strength of one current product or service compared to other offerings in your line. This exercise is not limited to business situations; it can be used to help make a variety of decisions in life, including things like buying a house or evaluating career opportunities.

The example that follows describes how WOW Pest Control developed the "Ideal Attributes" to be used in helping them make objective and informed decisions regarding their current market segment, and three potential new opportunities that were identified during the "SWOT" analysis portion of their strategic planning exercise. Not only does the example describe how they arrived at the "Ideal Attributes," but it also shows the actual results after they applied those evaluation criteria to compare their current market segment (residential pest control in Miller County) to the other three potential opportunities.

The "Ideal Attributes" Tool, as Applied to WOW Pest Control's Strategic Decision Process

In the "Ideal Attributes" exercise, each current and potential product/market segment is scored using ideal attributes and weights *determined by the leadership of the organization*. The decision is then made regarding which segment(s) will be allotted time, people, and money to pursue. Some existing products/markets might be dropped, while some potential new products/markets might score high enough to be added. The company can still choose to take business in other product/market segments if there is available capacity, but the sole focus of resources will be on the ones that meet the criteria.

To illustrate how this works, the leadership team of WOW Pest Control chose the four "Ideal Attributes" listed below, and then assigned different weights to each of the four attributes based on their relative importance. They could have selected whatever weights they preferred, provided the total did not exceed 100 percent. Similarly, they could have selected fewer than, or more than, four attributes (although, for simplicity, it is recommended that there never be more than six). **Note that the leadership team also agreed an opportunity must score at least 3.2 out of 4 to warrant further study.**

Ideal Attribute #1 – Degree to which it fits with company's long-term Vision and Mission (Weight = 35%):

4 = Fits perfectly with our long-term Vision and Mission

3 = Fits strongly with our long-term Vision and Mission

2 = Fits moderately with our long-term Vision and Mission

1 = Fits minimally with our long-term Vision and Mission

0 = Does not fit with our long-term Vision and Mission

Ideal Attribute #2 – Degree to which we could be "first choice" in this product/market segment within three years (Weight = 30%):

4 = We could become the "first choice" in this product/market segment within three years

3 = We could become ranked second or third in this product/market segment within three years

2 = We could become ranked fourth or fifth in this product/market segment within three years

1 = We could become ranked sixth to tenth in this product/market segment within three years

0 = We could become ranked eleventh or worse in this product/market segment within three years

Ideal Attribute #3 – Projected gross profit percentage for this product/market segment (Weight = 20%):

4 = Projected gross profit of 50% or more

3 = Projected gross profit of 40% to 49%

2 = Projected gross profit of 30% to 39%

1 = Projected gross profit of 20% to 29%

0 = Projected gross profit of less than 20%

Ideal Attribute #4 – Projected annual growth rate for this product/market segment (Weight = 15%):

4 = Projected growth rate of 20% or more per year

3 = Projected growth rate of 15% to 19% per year

2 = Projected growth rate of 10% to 14% per year

1 = Projected growth rate of 5% to 9% per year

0 = Projected growth rate of less than 5% per year

See next page for an explanation of how WOW Pest Control used these Ideal Attributes during their strategic planning process.

Ideal Attributes: Scores for Current and Potential Products/Markets – WOW Pest Control

The leadership team identified three potential opportunities as part of their strategic planning process. The three opportunities are listed in the table below, in addition to the current market/product served by the company. Using the ideal attributes, weights, and scoring method selected by leaders of WOW Pest Control, each of the three opportunities was thoroughly researched, evaluated, and scored to arrive at the results below. For comparison purposes, the current market/product segment was also scored, and is included below.

	Fit with Vision and Mission	+ Could Capture High Mkt Rank	+ Gross Profit %	+ Growth Rate	= IDEAL ATTRIBUTES SCORE
CURRENT OFFERINGS:					
Residential Pest Control In Miller County	(4)x(.35)	(4)x(.30)	(4)x(.20)	(2)x(.15)	**3.70**
POSSIBLE NEW OPPORTUNITIES:					
Lawn Chemicals to Current Miller County Customers	(1)x(.35)	(2)x(.30)	(4)x(.20)	(2)x(.15)	**2.05**
Provide Pest Control Svc. to Miller County Businesses	(1)x(.35)	(2)x(.30)	(2)x(.20)	(3)x(.15)	**1.80**
Expand Residential Pest Control to Casper County	(4)x(.35)	(2)x(.30)	(4)x(.20)	(2)x(.15)	**3.10**

**DECISION BASED ON THE ABOVE ANALYSIS: Since the company had set a <u>minimum score of 3.2 out 4</u> to qualify for further consideration, not a single potential opportunity met the minimum score, although one fell short by a very small margin (expand residential pest control service to Casper County) and may justify consideration during the next planning cycle to see if any facts may have changed, thereby increasing the score to 3.2 or higher.

While the preceding example demonstrates how a company might evaluate current and potential products or market segments, the same process can be used for a variety of other applications. Many organizations use the Ideal Attributes process to evaluate their current customers. For example, they may choose attributes like how quickly customers pay invoices (perhaps a score of 4 would identify customers who pay in 10 days or less, and a score of zero would be assigned to those who fail to pay within 90 days). Other attributes often used to evaluate current customers include: geographic proximity (how close they are to your location), gross profit margin, average size of each order, total annual purchases, or how easy or difficult they are to deal with on a regular basis.

If an existing customer scores low after going through this exercise, it does not mean that you need to fire that customer. However, it is often good to ask, "Under what conditions will we continue to do business with this customer?" In certain cases, it may be that you must gradually increase prices and let the customer decide if it still makes sense to buy from you; if they choose to no longer do business with you, it's their decision, not yours, but be prepared to let them walk away.

Here's one quick piece of advice about your cost and your selling price. The market price is determined by what the customer is willing to pay for your product or service, not what it costs you to make that product or deliver that service. If a customer is willing to pay $5.00 for your product, but it only costs you $1.00 to make it, don't under-price it at $2.00. Similarly, if it costs you $6.00 to make it, but the customer is still only willing to pay $5.00 for it, either figure out a way to make it less expensively, or stop trying to sell it.

One business owner applied the Ideal Attributes logic to developing price quotes. In his business, essentially every product he manufactures is made to the unique specifications of the customer. Since no two jobs are alike, he had always felt like he needed to maintain control of quoting to make certain there were no errors. He would start by adding labor, materials, and overhead, plus a mark-up of 30 percent. Then we would increase the price to account for other factors that he knew should be included based on his previous experience before quoting his final price.

As the business grew, he realized that he no longer had the time to do all the quoting himself. He knew he could rely on others in his company to accurately calculate labor, materials, overhead, and then add 30 percent, but what about all of the additional factors he applied to each quote based entirely on his own experience? It was then that he decided to develop a formal list of everything that needed to be considered, and to place a value on each of those factors. These were the same factors that he had long been applying as he quoted each project, but had never committed to paper. They included things like whether or not this was a "rush" project, problems that could possibly occur due to some special ingredient or material that was required to manufacture the product, and how difficult this customer is to deal with before, during, and after the sale. Based on the answers to these questions, he would add various percentage points to the 30 percent mark-up. For example, after applying the methodology above, the quote might have a mark-up of 42 percent instead of 30 percent. By quantifying his own logic, others in his company could now complete the vast majority of quotes without his intervention, and they began to understand his thought process as well.

This exercise can also be used to make decisions in your personal life, and it can be done more simply than the detailed example we just presented. You can use a basic ranking process instead, although it will be less precise. The following example demonstrates how this can be done when buying a house.

Simplified Ideal Attributes Example, Using the Ranking Method: Buying a New House

Assume you are evaluating five prospective houses to determine which one makes the most sense for your family, and you have selected six Ideal Attributes to use in arriving at a decision: drive-time to work, proximity to good schools, resale value, ease of adding-on if necessary, listing price, and upkeep. You then simply rank the five properties from most ideal (1) to least ideal (5) based on those attributes, as shown below:

	Property A	Property B	Property C	Property D	Property E
Drive time to work	2	4	5	1	3
Proximity to good schools	1	3	4	5	2
Resale value	5	3	2	4	1
Ease of adding-on later	3	2	1	5	4
Price	2	4	1	3	5
Regular upkeep required	1	5	2	4	3
TOTAL	**14**	**21**	**15**	**22**	**18**

The objective in the above exercise is to choose the house that has the lowest cumulative score (that is, the most ideal would be a total score of six, since that would mean that the house was ranked as first in all six categories). Therefore, in the example above, Property A scores the best (14) based on the attributes and rankings that were used.

Step 3: Analyze the Environmental Factors at Work in the Marketplace

(See Sample Plan at the End of this Chapter)

This is the part of the planning process that is frequently omitted or done very poorly, and the result is a strategic plan that is nothing more than **a waste of time, effort, and expense**. The objective is to IDENTIFY THE REALITY that affects the organization every day. These are things that are outside of your control, both positive and negative, that must be dealt with over the planning period. Examples are: general economic conditions, success or failure of competitors (both new and old), competitive pricing, demographic shifts that affect your customers/markets, changes in government regulations, availability of qualified employees, or changes in technology. If you compete in more than one market segment, this exercise should be completed separately for each of those segments. In the case of WOW Pest Control, through the "Ideal Attributes" exercise they determined that none of the three potential new products/ markets met the minimum score they had established, so you will note in the sample plan at the end of this chapter that they have conducted the environmental analysis on only the business segment where they currently participate. If one of the potential new products/ markets had met their minimum criteria, they would have conducted a separate analysis of environmental factors for that new product/market as well.

It is absolutely essential that this information be unbiased and supported by as much documentation as possible, often from industry or government sources that are taking a realistic view of the future. The business owner is generally too close to the situation to objectively and realistically evaluate these factors and their expected impact on the business.

Assuming the facts have been gathered accurately and thoroughly, the final step is to take an overall look at those facts and try to draw some conclusions from them. These will serve as your **key planning assumptions** when determining what you will need to do in an effort to mitigate negative factors, and take advantage of opportunities that might be available to you in the market.

Included in key assumptions are certain other prequalifiers or non-negotiable factors that may be important to the business owner on a personal level, including things like, "We will not sell the business," or "We will not make any acquisitions, since it could jeopardize our culture if we tried to combine a vastly different culture with our own."

It's important to pause here for a moment to emphasize that **the environment changes regularly, and those changes often require modification of the plan. This is where "WOW!" companies turn traditional strategic** plans into a *perpetual planning process* by making those modifications immediately, versus "getting caught" by undetected changes in the environment that will render their plan less effective or obsolete.

Step 4: Identify Strengths, Weaknesses, Opportunities, and Threats – "SWOT" Analysis

(See Sample Plan at the End of this Chapter)

The SWOT analysis must also be done separately for each market segment in which you compete. While you may have a great strength in one market segment, that strength often means nothing to customers in another segment where you compete.

My personal preference is to limit the number of strengths, weaknesses, opportunities, and threats to no more than three each. While you may be tempted to start with a laundry list of strengths, deeper evaluation will reveal that most of the items listed are the *results* of some underlying strengths rather than being strengths in-and-of themselves. For example, if your company has a great reputation, it is probably the result of some other basic strength that you possess. Maybe it's the quality of your work compared to other competitors. If you consider your employees to be great, there is likely something that your people do better than those employed by your competitors, like their responsiveness.

By truly focusing on this exercise, some companies have been able to identify an underlying strength which is so unique and strong that it could actually be transferred to an entirely different business. This is generally referred to as a *core competency*. For example, one company did an almost unbelievable job of providing employees with the very best employee training and development. The owner was so passionate about developing employees that the company could easily have gone into a totally unrelated business with different employees, and the new employees would quickly be the most highly trained people in the new industry because the owner would be absolutely and totally focused on bringing the very best available development to the employees. At another company, the employees were so genuinely pumped-up about serving their customers that they continually came up with innovative ways that far surpassed anyone in their industry. These same people could likely duplicate this feat in an entirely different environment.....that's how a core competency works, and why so few companies truly have one.

So dig deeply when going through this exercise. The objective is to find the one, two, or three factors that make you better than your competitor (differentiators), or worse (in the case of key underlying weaknesses that you may have identified).

Opportunities are generally things that are available to you outside of your company, like a new market that might be ripe for your entry. However, there are occasionally some opportunities that are internal, like selling off old equipment to help finance the launch of a new product. When new opportunities are available the "Ideal Attributes" tool is an excellent way to score and rank them.

Threats are things which are outside of your control, like the rising prices of a key raw material used in your product that could jeopardize your business, or a vendor who decides to circumvent your company and begin selling directly to your customers. If you have done the environmental analysis well (from Step 3), you have probably already identified the key threats during that exercise. Please note that there is often a tendency to list things as threats which are actually weaknesses, so when you have your list of threats identified, ask yourself if these things are *truly* outside of your control. If not, they are weaknesses that should have been identified as such.

Step 5: Revisit the Organizational Vision

Note that this is the time to pause for a moment and take a fresh look at the Vision for your organization to make sure it is still realistic in view of the future reality that you have just described in Steps 3 and 4. If your vision is too aggressive, or not aggressive enough, based on the outlook, then it should be modified appropriately.

Step 6: Identify the Key Issues to be Addressed

(See Sample Plan at the End of this Chapter)

Business owners are often surprised that most of the time and effort in the planning process is devoted to all the "preparatory" things described in the first five steps, but the real planning doesn't actually start until the Key Issues are identified. It is at this point that the planning team reviews all of the previous steps to identify the one, two, or three things that are absolutely crucial in order to stay on track with the Vision (remember that the Vision is the ideal state, or the clearly-defined end point, regardless of how many years in the future it might be).

Key Issues are called different things by different people. Regardless of what label they've been given, they are typically weaknesses that must be fixed, or opportunities that are to be pursued. They can be short-term issues that are more operational in nature, or long-term issues that are more strategic. The first time an organization plans, most of the Key Issues come from the list of weaknesses, since it's very difficult to take advantage of the opportunities until those obstacles are addressed. However, as the perpetual planning process is implemented, the company is more and more able to focus its efforts on taking advantage of strategic opportunities, since most weaknesses will already have been addressed.

Step 7: Establish Quantitative Expectations for Each Key Issue

(See Sample Plan at the End of this Chapter)

One of the most critical steps in identifying the Key Issues is to also determine *how you will know when you have adequately addressed each issue.* That is, what outcome will have occurred to prove that the problem is behind you, or that you have successfully taken advantage of the opportunity? For example, if the Key Issue is "Customer Turnover," then you may want to set some expectations for twelve, twenty-four, or thirty-six months, measured by either "% of Customers Lost," or by a more positive measure, "% of Customers Retained." Note that I prefer using the word "expectations" when setting these measures, since it conveys the idea that these truly are expected outcomes, not pie-in-the-sky goals or objectives. That said, be sure to make the expectations realistic in terms of both quantity and timeframe, and make it perfectly clear that these truly ARE expectations with accountability attached to them. *Meeting* the expectation does not bring a reward, since that's what employees are already being paid to do; instead, rewards come from *exceeding* the expectation.

You will see in the WOW Pest Control plan that time-related, quantitative expectations have been established for each Key Issue. Chapter Six will provide details regarding the creation of incentive compensation plans for individual employees who are responsible for these measures so they will be rewarded when expectations are exceeded.

Step 8: Create Action Plans, Due Dates, and Assign Responsibility

(See Sample Plan at the End of this Chapter)

This step is fairly straight-forward. The purpose is to put teeth into the plan by identifying each major step that must be completed in order to address the Key Issue and achieve the quantitative, time-related expectation. Then, assign a qualified and capable individual to each step, and determine a realistic date when the step must be completed.

There are two basic rules for this exercise. First, try not to put more than one name next to any action item, even if others may be assisting the person whose name appears on the line. Unless one person has the full responsibility for that action item, it will be difficult to assign accountability. Keep in mind that the person whose name is on the line has the right to get help from anyone in the organization, including someone who may be "higher ranking" than the person whose name is on the line. Secondly, resist the urge to pick due dates that are too aggressive; in fact, encourage people to set due dates they truly believe they can meet.

Step 9: Allocate Resources to Accomplish the Action Plans

It is at this point that the necessary resources are allocated to make sure that the plan can be implemented. That means setting aside the necessary funding. For example, if the plan calls for hiring additional employees or purchasing equipment, those funds need to be part of budgets and forecasts over the planning horizon. If there is not adequate funding available, it may be necessary to modify the plan, or to implement it over a longer time horizon to make it "affordable." Remember that you can't hold people responsible for implementing a plan if you have not allocated the resources that will allow them to do what you've asked of them.

Step 10: Establish and Adhere to a Regular Planning Review Process

Here is where many good plans fail. Businesses spend a great deal of time and energy to create a plan, including the "accountability" of expected outcomes, action items, due dates, and assignment of people who are responsible. Yet, there is no accountability in the review process. **If you want to have a perpetual planning process, regular review is the key, since this is precisely what turns it into a _perpetual process!_**

Also remember this important ingredient for success. **If the leader of the organization does not relentlessly drive the process, it won't happen.** The first time a review meeting is cancelled, it sends a signal that the day-to-day planning process is no longer a top priority of the owner/leader. If you are not going to drive the review process RELENTLESSLY, then don't waste the time and energy to plan!

What does a typical review process look like? It's important to get into a realistic "rhythm" regarding the review process. The rhythm for a company that is growing at 30 percent per year is often different from the rhythm of a company that is growing at 5 percent per year. For example, in an organization where growth is rapid and the competitive landscape is changing quickly, the right "rhythm" for planning review meetings might be weekly, or even more frequently than that. For organizations that are growing at more moderate rates in industries that are more stable, monthly review meetings might be more appropriate. You'll need to determine your own "rhythm." The right answer is to meet as frequently as necessary to maintain it as a process, rather than a project, yet not so frequently that the meetings become a waste of time.

Once you determine the rhythm, remember to keep the meetings as brief and focused as possible. Expect every member of your team to report on the progress and current status of each action item, and encourage them to ask for help if they need it rather than possibly falling behind on a due date. You don't want any unpleasant surprises later.

What Can You Reasonably Expect from Planning?

During the first year of planning you are likely to find that most of the due dates are within the first twelve months, and that you've probably created nothing more than a one-year operational plan and budget. This is NORMAL! Although you might not view this as strategic, you've actually made huge progress toward thinking more strategically and longer term. In the second year, you will find that you have a much better understanding of the environmental factors affecting your business, including your competition, and you'll realize that you've successfully addressed many of the internal weaknesses that may have been holding you back. In addition, the due dates will tend to be a little further out as you begin to move toward a more strategic perspective. By the third year, you'll feel in control of your business, and hopefully will have adopted planning as a process, not a project.

The key to implementing the plan is commitment by the leader, including regularly scheduled review meetings where each person takes full responsibility for the action items and due dates assigned to them!

Sample Strategic Plan – WOW Pest Control, Inc.

NOTE: The Personal Vision is not included as part of the strategic plan, since it is a very private exercise, and the results of that exercise could include information that would not be appropriate to share with employees. For more details, see Step 1 of this chapter.

Vision (very specifically defines what we someday want to become, written in the future tense, and designed to motivate and provide clarity to employees)

"WOW Pest Control will be the first choice for residential pest control services in Miller County."

(Key points for our employees to understand: While we may occasionally accept business outside of Miller County, we will focus all of our time, people, and money to serve residential customers in Miller County. If we ever decide to serve another county, we will proactively pursue that county only if there is a high probability that we will eventually become the first choice for residential pest control services. Although we will periodically review our Vision to make sure it remains appropriate, we will remain exclusively in the residential market until there is enough compelling evidence for us to consider something different. In conjunction with our local university, we will conduct market surveys every two years to determine our progress toward becoming "first choice," and will share this progress with employees.)

Mission (describes what we do, and for whom)

"WOW Pest Control provides comprehensive, high-quality, environmentally safe pest control services to homeowners in Miller County."

Values and Beliefs

We absolutely guarantee our customers that no other pest control service in Miller County will provide better quality or more timely service............period.

We will always use environmentally safe materials and be on the leading edge of eco-friendly pest control solutions and technology.

We will be relentless in providing the greatest customer care in our industry.

Our future success will be largely the result of unsolicited referrals from current customers who truly value our service.

Our employees will be the most technically trained in the pest control industry to protect the health and well-being of the customers we serve, and the environment in which we live.

Each and every employee will always operate in a safe working environment, and with the most technologically advanced equipment available.

Key Environmental Factors (Positive & Negative) That Will Affect the Industry in the Next Three Years

Although the local economy will recover slowly, it will result in the gradual increase of disposable income of residential customers in Miller County.

Industry pricing will continue to be competitive in our market area.

There will be continued consolidation of competitors in our industry.

Residential property owners with higher incomes will continue to be less affected by economic pressures, and be more apt to continue or initiate pest control services than those with lower incomes.

The cost of environmentally friendly chemicals will continue to rise faster than the general inflation rate.

The trend to environmentally friendly materials will accelerate due to governmental regulations.

The price of fuel will continue to increase.

Recruiting employees for the pest control industry will remain challenging.

The trend toward fewer English-speaking employees will continue.

Three Greatest Strengths (specific things that we do better, and differentiate us from competitors)

Most technically trained team in the industry.

Most responsive employees due to relentless customer focus.

Quality of our work, as evidenced by higher than average referral rate.

Three Greatest Weaknesses (areas where we need to improve, or where a competitor is better)

Recruiting, developing, and training employees to fuel our growth.

Marketing, since we have not leveraged our stellar customer reputation with the community at large.

Equipment in need of repair or replacement.

Three Greatest Opportunities

Provide lawn chemical applications to current residential pest control customers.

Take on commercial pest control customers in our current market area of Miller County.

Expand residential pest control service to Casper County.

NOTE: As shown earlier in this chapter, the WOW Pest Control planning team created a set of "Ideal Attributes" to be used in evaluating potential opportunities, and established a minimum score that must be met if an opportunity is to receive further consideration. None of the three opportunities listed above achieved the minimum score, although one of them came close and will be evaluated again during the next planning cycle.

Three Greatest Threats

Chemical prices could increase substantially, especially environmentally friendly materials.

Further consolidation in our market could create a huge competitor.

New, small competitors could enter the market and drive prices down due to their low overhead.

KEY STRATEGIC ISSUES (no more than three)

Issue 1 – Recruiting, Developing, and Retaining Stellar Employees
Issue 2 – Marketing as a Strategy for Sales Growth

ISSUE 1: RECRUITING, DEVELOPING, AND RETAINING STELLAR EMPLOYEES

EXPECTATIONS

KEY MEASURES OF SUCCESS	Current Yr	Yr 1 of Plan	Yr 2 of Plan	Yr 3 of Plan
% of Open Jobs Filled Within 14 Days	62%	68%	75%	83%
% of Employees Who Leave Within 45 Days	24%	21%	18%	15%
% of Employees Who Stay More Than 1 Yr	58%	62%	66%	70%
% of Employees Who Pass WOW Training Test	N.A.	50%	65%	80%

ACTION STEPS	Assigned to	Completed by
1. Develop relationships with local high schools to attract candidates	Emma	3/30, Yr 1
2. Recruit two supervisors who can speak Spanish	Emma	6/30, Yr 1
3. Find consultant to recommend assessment screening test for hiring	Jose	1/31, Yr 2
4. Assign a mentor to each new employee for first three months	Jose	1/31, Yr 2
5. Create a WOW training program, and a "pass/fail" test	Patrick	9/30, Yr 1
6. Acquire equipment to enhance employee safety and productivity	Jose	2/28, Yr 3
7. Conduct exit interviews to determine why employees leave company	Emma	On-Going

ISSUE 2: MARKETING AS A STRATEGY FOR SALES GROWTH

EXPECTATIONS

KEY MEASURES OF SUCCESS	Current Yr	Yr 1 of Plan	Yr 2 of Plan	Yr 3 of Plan
% Increase in Website Visits vs. Prior Year	N.A.	+25%	+30%	+35%
# of New Clients from Customer Referrals	35	80	140	225
Total Number of New Clients	75	130	210	315
% of Customers Retained from Prior Year	74%	79%	85%	92%

ACTION STEPS	Assigned to	Completed by
1. Find consultant to revise website & use search engine optimization	Howard	9/30, Yr 1
2. Develop documented process for following-up website leads	Howard	2/28, Yr 2
3. Create new program to generate referrals from current customers	Will	4/30, Yr 2
4. Develop incentive comp plan to drive customer referrals	Will	4/30, Yr 2
5. Develop incentive comp plan to reward customer retention	Howard	1/31, Yr 3

CHAPTER 4

The Second **"P"**

PEOPLE Who "Fit,"
Today & Tomorrow

The Second **"P"**

PEOPLE Who "Fit," Today & Tomorrow

Only after a company has a strong planning process in place can it develop an organization that is qualified to implement the plan. In this chapter we will describe Steps 11 through 17, all of them crucial to successfully executing the strategy.

It has often been said that structure follows strategy, not the reverse. However, many business owners try to forge ahead with a plan using the wrong structure, the wrong skill sets, or both, simply because it's difficult and sometimes painful to make "people changes."

To demonstrate how important it is that structure follows strategy, consider the basketball team who is confronted with two different game situations—*trailing* by two points with five seconds on the clock and about to throw the ball inbounds for a shot to tie or win the game, versus *leading* by five points with twenty seconds on the clock and about to throw the ball inbounds to run-out the clock. Clearly, the plans are dramatically different in each of those two situations—perhaps setting-up a quick and uncontested shot in the first case, and running-out the clock in the second case. To execute either of the two plans, the positioning of the players on the court (organization structure) will be significantly different, and the skill sets needed in each of those positions will be different. It may require putting your best shooters on the floor in the first case, and your best ball-handlers and free-throw shooters in the second case.

Step 11: Determine the Organizational Structure Needed

The "right" structure and the "right" skill sets in a business organization must be determined by the Vision, and then by the plan that has been created to achieve that Vision. While many businesses are willing to change the structure/organizational chart to align with the plan, they fail to fill that structure with the skill sets they need to *implement* the plan.

This is not an easy task, and it's one that I wrestled with during my own career. In fact, the most objective and accurate way to determine what skills will be required in the future is to first assume that you have no current employees. As you go through this exercise, imagine that you've been called-in as a consultant to create the ideal organizational chart and ideal candidates to fill each high-level management position. It's often easier to build your new organizational chart if you have some blank large sticky notes so that you can write on them, and then move them around as you think through the process. Also, be sure to have a camera so you can photograph various scenarios for future reference.

Begin by arranging the sticky notes to show your current organizational chart, but do not go beyond the top-tier jobs—those who report directly to you. Note that this process can be repeated later for the remainder of positions in your organization, but you must first focus on those at the top. List only the "function" on each sticky note, not the title or the name of the person currently holding that position. Here's an example:

Current Organizational Structure...

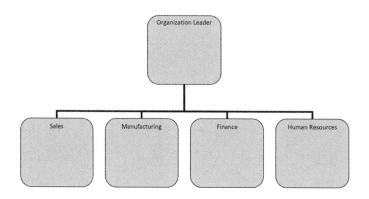

Now, take a close look at your new strategic plan and determine what structure will be necessary to successfully achieve it. Remember that in some cases the organizational structure might actually still be appropriate if the strategy hasn't changed dramatically. For the sake of example, let's assume the organization has been a manufacturer of products for many years, but has now decided that only a portion of the product line will continue to be made in the company's facilities, while the other portion will be made off-shore by other companies, a significant departure from the way production has been handled in the past. In addition, sales efforts will now include the traditional model of calling on distributors, plus the new strategic focus of selling to certain market segments strictly through the internet.

Based on these changes, the company has determined that the following organizational structure will be required, so new large sticky notes should now be arranged in the manner shown in the next diagram. Please note that there must be total clarity when creating the organizational chart, with no employee having more than one boss, no overlap, and no duplication. It's also essential that there be a succession plan for key positions, including the leader, to make certain that the organization doesn't become vulnerable if a crucial employee exits for any reason, intentionally or unintentionally.

Future Organizational Structure.....

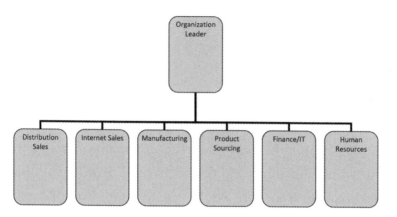

Step 12: Identify Skill Sets Needed in Each Position

In taking the next steps, do your best to forget about every employee who is already part of the organization, including the leader/owner. Only after you've completed this exercise should you look at the "inventory" of people who already work for the organization.

Using the future organizational structure above, now record the following information on each sticky note—the primary duties and responsibilities of each position (not more than the few key items), and the profile of the ideal candidate to fill each position (your "wish list" of education, experience, etc...). Again, you should only be focused on the top-tier positions at this point, since this same procedure can be done later with the remaining jobs, many of which will have also changed due to the new strategic plan.

It's important to note here that the business owner also needs to periodically monitor whether or not he or she is still qualified to lead the organization forward. Being the owner does not necessarily qualify you to lead the organization effectively! One of the best methods of determining whether or not your own leadership skills still qualify you to run the organization is to rely on your Outside Board for their candid input as your company grows. More will be said about Outside Boards in Chapter 7, but it's also important to mention it here because having people who fit, today and tomorrow, should include outside advisors who provide skill sets your business needs. These are experts you could probably never afford to hire as employees, but who can offer you guidance in areas that are critical to your future success. **Like any other member of your organization, as the needs of your business change, the members of your Board must change periodically as well.**

Step 13: Create/Update Job Descriptions

After determining the primary duties and responsibilities for each position, then create detailed job descriptions, and repeat the procedure for every position in the organization. If you don't have a good format to follow, contact a professional to assist you, or go online and find a format you like. Remember that it will be very difficult to evaluate an employee's performance later if you have not clearly defined the duties and expectations through an accurate and up-to-date job description.

Step 14: Assess Current Employees to Determine Who Fits

Now it's time to look through your current employees to see which ones will fit immediately, which ones might fit with some development, and which ones will not fit as the organization changes to accomplish your plan. At the conclusion of the exercise (assuming you have been truly objective), you will have defined what it takes to have a stellar performer in each position, including the top leadership role.

Whether you use large sticky notes, a white board, or some other technique that works for you, the exercise above is something that should be done at least annually as you look at your upcoming three or five-year plan, and the skill sets that will be required in each position if your organization is going to achieve that plan and, ultimately, your Vision.

There are a few very important factors to consider when evaluating competency of any employee, regardless of their position in the organization. Some business owners may have had very limited exposure to a stellar performer before starting the business. For example, it is not uncommon to find a business owner who has a Chief Financial Officer who is believed to be a top performer *"because he/she is the very best financial person I've ever met."* Nevertheless, a seasoned outsider might immediately recognize that the CFO is simply a great bookkeeper who is better than any other bookkeeper that the business owner has ever encountered. In other words, the business owner's frame of reference is limited by his or her previous exposure to "financial" people.

Step 15: Establish a Budget for Training and Development

Over time, a strong performer can decline to average, or even below average performance. Why? The complexity of the jobs will grow as the company grows, and the company will often outgrow the skill sets of its employees. If the skills and competencies of the employees stand still, so will the company. That's why "WOW!" companies set aside funds that are specifically earmarked for employee development, and aggressively invest in those employees so they reach their full potential.

Step 16: Create Individual Development Plans for Each Employee

The responsibility for employee development lies with two parties. On the one hand, the business owner carries the responsibility to provide training and development so that each employee reaches his or her full potential, and on the other hand, the employee bears the responsibility of continuing to learn and develop in order to operate at a performance level that increases with the growth of the organization. When either party fails to accept this responsibility, or the employee simply doesn't have the God-given talents to develop any further, the organization's growth will be inhibited. In other words, without focusing the proper attention on employee development, in a growing company a top performer can become average, or even sub-par.

The obvious question is, "Do I have to terminate every employee whose performance doesn't measure-up to expectations?" The answer is that it's always great to keep people who "fit" your culture if you can make it work, but if their full competency and potential has been reached and there's no capacity for improvement, it may be time to move those employees to other less demanding roles that are still within their competency levels. While that typically involves a demotion or, at the very least, no further promotions, it's the right thing to do. It just needs to be done with fairness and dignity. It's surprising how many of those employees are actually grateful to have been relieved of job duties that they already knew they couldn't perform satisfactorily. After the move, that same employee might actually become a strong performer again in a new lower-level role that is more appropriately aligned with his or her skill set. **If you want to avoid demoting or terminating people later, then you simply have to do a better job of regularly evaluating individual skill sets to avoid putting people in positions where they will likely fail!**

Leadership Competency: A Great Predictor of Progress Toward "WOW!"

Over the years, I've had the pleasure of facilitating countless strategic planning meetings for privately-held companies. In most cases, the planning team consisted of the owner(s) and key managers/VP's who reported directly to the owner(s). That was when I first recognized that the majority of those companies had some people in the room who should not have been there because they lacked the required skill sets, the right attitude, or both. This issue became so prevalent that I often recommended to the business owner that certain members of the planning team be professionally assessed by an outside organizational development consultant to determine if they actually had the skills and competencies to carry the business forward. After all, what good would it do to create a great strategic plan for an organization that didn't have the leadership skills to implement it?

There are some occasions when an employee who has long been stuck in a particular role can pleasantly surprise an organization by demonstrating a much higher level of leadership capability than previously believed possible, particularly if that employee is moved to a new environment that encourages personal leadership development. In other words, sometimes employees are conditioned to believe that they have limited talent and upside potential. It reminds me of an experiment I once saw in a film called *The Pike Syndrome* (details of the experiment can still be found on the Internet). The pike is a large fish that lives by eating smaller fish. In the experiment, the pike was first placed in a large tank by itself. After a period of time, smaller fish were introduced into the tank, but they were protected by a piece of glass that separated them from the pike. The pike repeatedly attempted to pursue the smaller fish, but was unsuccessful due to the glass barrier. Eventually, the pike gave up and stopped pursuing the other fish. It was then that the glass barrier was removed. While there was no longer a barrier, the pike never pursued the fish again and eventually starved to death, even though the small fish swam right next to it. Why? The pike had been conditioned to believe that the fish were not available to eat. In much the same way, some employees are conditioned to believe they are incapable of rising to higher levels of performance, or advancing in an organization, even though they have the skills to do so. By putting those employees in a working environment that encourages them to advance, you may find they can be proactively **developed** to fulfill leadership roles within an organization.

When business owners intentionally and aggressively devote more time to evaluating and developing the leadership skills of their team members before tackling a strategic planning process, the likelihood of creating and implementing a truly great plan increases dramatically.

If you're a business owner who has done an effective job of selecting and developing employees, and have been pleased with the stellar performance of some of your key people, you might be tempted to offer them "real" stock in your company. If you do, be aware that it can present major issues later when the employee leaves, either voluntary or involuntary. Here are just a few of the questions that typically arise:

- "What is the value of the shares of our privately-held company?"

- "Is the value per share different for a minority shareholder?

- "Does the employee have to sell them back to the company at the time they leave?"

- "Can the employee keep the shares, or pass them on to a family member, even though he or she no longer works for the company?

- "Must the shares be purchased by the company, in-full, immediately, or is there a scheduled pay-out?"

Instead of offering "real stock", consider a non-stock deferred compensation plan that provides many of the same advantages without relinquishing any ownership or control.

Non-stock deferred compensation plans have become increasingly popular among privately-held businesses as a method of rewarding those who are making major contributions to the growth of the enterprise.

These type plans are often incorrectly assumed to be real stock, since they're sometimes called "phantom stock" or "stock appreciation rights." However, they have no bearing on ownership, and have no voting rights.

Regardless of what they might be called, they present a very attractive alternative to awarding "real" stock, especially for privately held businesses. While they are sometimes awarded to those who already own traditional shares of stock in the company, they are most often issued to those who are not shareholders.

The best way to describe them is through an example. Therefore, let's assume that Acme Company has 4 owners:

- Individual A owns 25% of the company's stock
- Individual B owns 25% of the company's stock

- Individual C owns 25% of the company's stock

- Individual D owns 25% of the company's stock

- Individual D is active in the business, while A, B, and C are not.

- In addition to Individual D, there are two other employees who play crucial roles in growing the business over the long term through their day-to-day contributions—Individual E, and Individual F.

In an effort to reward Individuals D, E, and F for their active roles in growing the business, let's assume the four shareholders agree that these three people should receive a long-term incentive for their performance. In addition to rewarding them for growing the company, it should be noted that these types of plans also tend to keep key employees from leaving (making them less likely to take a job with a competitor, or to start a business of their own).

In this example, Shareholders A, B, and C agree to share 30% of the growth in the VALUE of the business (not sales, but true value) with Individuals D, E, and F. Here's how it would work.........First, the shareholders would agree on the value of the business on the date that the three employees begin the deferred compensation plan. Usually a formula is used to determine the value of the business, since that same formula can then be applied at a later date to calculate the actual dollar growth in the value of the business. Value is often calculated using a multiple of EBITDA (earnings before interest, taxes, depreciation, and amortization). Multiples vary depending on the industry and other factors, but a multiple of 3 or 4 is common.

Let's say that the value of the business, as calculated on 12/31/17, is $1 million. And, let's assume that Individual D is awarded a stake of 15%, Individual E receives 10%, and Individual F gets 5% (for a total of 30%). If the business is sold for $4 million in 2023, here's what would happen:

- Individual D would get 15% of the difference between $1 mill & $4 mill (.15 X $3 mill = $450K)

- Individual E would get 10% of the difference between $1 mill & $4 mill (.10 x $3 mill = $300K)

- Individual F would get 5% of the difference between $1 mill & $4 mill (.05 x $3 mill = $150K)

A total of $900,000 would be paid to the three individuals who are enrolled in the plan, generally at the time the deal is closed. Tax laws are always changing, but typically the distributions made to individuals under these agreements would be treated as ordinary income. The remaining $3.1 million ($4 million, less $900 thousand) would then be distributed to the 4 owners, as shown below:

- Individual A gets $775K (25% of the stock)

- Individual B gets $775K (25% of the stock)

- Individual C gets $775K (25% of the stock)

- Individual D gets $775K (25% of the stock)

Note that in the example above, Individual D would receive $775K for his ownership share in the company, as well as $450K for his deferred compensation award. The difference is that $775K would be subject to capital gains tax, whereas $450K would be treated as ordinary income. NOTE: DO NOT SET-UP A DEFERRED COMPENSATION PLAN WITHOUT THE HELP OF YOUR ATTORNEY AND TAX ADVISOR!

It's extremely important to emphasize that there are countless ways to structure non-stock deferred compensation agreements. The plan needs to be customized to deliver the kinds of objectives you want to achieve, and the type of behavior you want to reward. The purpose of these plans is to reward key players almost as if they were shareholders, yet no shares ever change hands. The absence of this type of incentive plan can lead to the departure of a key player, either to join a competitor, or to start a new business that will compete head-on.

The percentage set aside for deferred compensation plans can vary substantially. It's also important to remember that, if the company in the example decided to do so, they could reward another 10% at a later date, either to one of the three individuals who already received them, or to a new key player who joins the company. Of course, the value of those would be calculated using the formula at the time those new awards were granted (for example, the new starting point might be $2 million rather than $1 million).

Generally, these awards are granted on a particular date, but are vested over a period of time. For example, the 10% granted to Individual E would normally be vested as follows: 2% at the end of year one, 4% at the end of year two, 6% at the end of year three, 8% at the end of year four, and 10% at the end of year five. If the company is sold before the five-year vesting period, many companies will immediately vest them in full.

One other aspect to consider is the departure of a key employee who is part of this plan. In that event, the company calculates the value of the employee's award on the date that he or she leaves (based on the pre-established formula), and pays-out the funds over some period of time, perhaps 36 months, at a reasonable interest rate that has been established in the initial agreement.

This is only an example used to demonstrate the major features of non-stock deferred compensation plans for key employees. When you select the attorney who is going to help you create this plan, be sure it is someone who is very well versed in establishing such programs, and that your attorney and tax advisor are BOTH working together to create the plan.

Step 17: Determine New Employees Needed, and Recruit

Attracting, retaining, and developing people who "fit" the organization is absolutely essential at every level of the business, and the key to maintaining a healthy culture. In addition to making totally certain that all employees have the required skill sets to implement the plan, each of those employees must also have the right **attitude**, and the leader of the organization needs to take a **proactive** approach toward developing those great employees after they've joined the company. That means **establishing a budget** for the development of employees, **evaluating their performance** at least annually in relation to their job descriptions, and jointly agreeing on a **personalized development plan for each employee** as an integral part of that performance appraisal process, supported and financed by the employee development budget.

Perhaps the greatest way to build the right team is to make fewer mistakes in the hiring process. An effective recruiting process includes multiple interviews and some sort of assessment test to determine "fit." If you do not have a strong process for effectively recruiting, screening, interviewing and testing prospective employees. get help from an expert to create a proces you can administer yourself.

Taking a proactive approach is a key step in building an engaged and enthusiastic team of people. To illustrate the type of positive energy that this can generate, I once had a neighbor whose dog met me at the edge of my backyard with a saliva-soaked tennis ball in its mouth. Clearly the dog wanted me to remove the ball and throw it, at which point he returned the ball to me and we repeated the cycle again, and again, and again. When the dog finally died, they buried the tennis ball and the dog in the same grave. Compare that behavior to another dog that rarely moves unless it's time to eat or go outside. Employees need to be excited and energetic like the first dog, proactively bringing new ideas and recommendations for change, versus the second dog that is comfortable with the status quo—sort of "retired in place," and sucking the energy out of the organization.

Still, it's not enough to simply assemble a group of employees who have great attitudes. Strong cultures must be managed; they don't happen on their own. Rather, they require a leader who **genuinely and consistently** demonstrates the company's values and beliefs, since it's the day-to-day behavior of the leader that truly sets the tone for the culture. It even manifests itself in the way the employee manual is written, generally in a much more positive tone, versus using a "thou shalt not" approach.

When visiting a business owner at his or her office for the first time, I'm often given a tour of the facilities. It's very enlightening to observe how each employee reacts when the business owner walks through the building. The body language of those employees provides great insight as to what it's really like to work there, regardless of the Vision, Mission, Values, Beliefs, or Pledge that might be posted prominently on the wall.

Every "WOW!" business I've encountered exhibits a great culture, without exception. This is no coincidence, since a company's culture is largely a reflection of the demonstrated behavior of the leader. This is exactly why turmoil exists when an organization with an otherwise great culture gets a new leader. Even though the company's values and beliefs might still be posted on the wall, the new leader might not be demonstrating those things every day. Unfortunately, too many organizations claim their employees are their most valuable asset, yet the owner has a reserved parking spot closest to the front door. We should never fail to remember that the culture of a privately-held organization is heavily influenced, both positively and negatively, by its leader!

One of the 'WOW!' companies I've had the pleasure of working with is Alternate Solutions Healthnet, headquartered in Dayton, Ohio, with operations in a variety of other cities as well. Owned and led by David and Tessie Ganzsarto, the company's culture is so exemplary and well-managed that I honestly can't adequately describe it in words. They actually publish a culture book each year, filled with full color photographs and letters from patients, their families, and employees themselves. Despite tremendous company growth, employees working away from the corporate headquarters, and a limited supply of available nurses and physical therapists, the company has won numerous awards and has potential employees waiting in line to work there. I'll talk more about Alternate Solutions Healthnet later, but suffice it to say that their culture is a managed process, driven by a leadership team who has genuine passion for being the very best provider of home health care services, and the greatest place in the industry for employees to work.

CHAPTER 5

The Third **"P"**

PROCESSES

The Third **"P"**

PROCESSES

While this chapter is short compared to others in this book, processes are no less important than planning, people, performetrics or passion. It's just difficult to get specific about this topic since every one of the companies I've worked with has different processes for different and valid reasons.

An organization may have hundreds, or even thousands, of processes. For example, there are likely many processes and sub-processes pertaining to sales, manufacturing, billings, collections, recruiting/hiring new employees, and countless other business activities. Yet, while every organization has processes, the degree to which they have control over those processes can vary widely.

Step 18: Evaluate/Revise Processes

The things that make the processes different at "WOW!" companies are as follows:

- They are in alignment with, and driven by, the company's strategic plan and initiatives.

- They are well-documented.
- They are clear, leaving no room for misinterpretation.
- They are repeatable.
- They are followed to the letter.
- Job descriptions are linked to them.
- Incentive compensation is linked to them.
- Employee training and development are built around them.
- They are continuously re-evaluated to make certain they are still the best processes in light of things that may have changed (customer demands, technology, competitive pressure, market pricing, etc...).
- Someone in the organization is fully responsible, either full or part-time, to make certain that all of the above requirements are being met.

The processes at a "WOW!" company are not limited to how people do their jobs day-to-day. They include everything from the way the company recruits new employees to the way they bid them farewell. There are specific and well-documented base pay ranges for each position that are tied to education, experience, and other factors, as well as clear policies and procedures that are spelled-out in the employee manual.

To organizations that are NOT in the "WOW!" category, the above may seem to be a daunting task. However, believe it or not, in "WOW!" companies this "P" is actually a logical outcome of the first two "P's," a perpetual planning process and people who are purpose-driven.

Why? The answer is simple. First, a perpetual planning process results in a very detailed to-do list for each and every employee in the organization, all tied to the expected outcomes specified in the plan. And second, the structure needed and people skills required to implement that plan include clear expectations for each job (as defined in the job description). So with all of these things already in place, determining the necessary *processes* is a very logical exercise.

One of the most dramatic process improvements I've ever encountered was in a manufacturing company that had just been blind-sided by foreign competition, resulting in the loss of more than 50 percent of their business due primarily to abrupt and significant drops in market pricing. The leader of the organization was absolutely and totally committed to become the most efficient manufacturer in the industry so that this would never occur again. He began by involving employees in the solution, aided by an outside consultant who was a process expert. The company began by videotaping one department in the factory to observe the current processes, and then had everyone in that department watch the videotape. They hated it! But they soon began to see how they could streamline processes and reduce costs by significantly more than they had originally targeted. In addition to the cost reductions, the employees found they were not working nearly as hard, but much smarter, with the result being a dramatic improvement in efficiency. As word spread across the plant, other departments wanted to be next! In less than two years, the total dollar sales per employee nearly tripled!

As demonstrated by the relentless drive of the leader in the real-life case above, the most challenging part about processes is making sure that someone in the organization is formally responsible and committed to overseeing them and making them better. In addition, it's crucial that there are purpose-driven people in the organization who have the necessary skill sets to recognize when the processes are becoming outdated or inefficient so that they can implement the changes necessary to keep them current.

Many companies have made great strides over the years in documenting their processes, particularly manufacturers who have achieved various "quality certifications" as prompted by their customers. The potential downside is that these well-documented processes often become inefficient or obsolete if not continuously monitored and improved to meet changing customer needs.

What are the signs that a company may have issues with their processes? Typical symptoms include customer complaints about quality, delivery, accuracy, or customer service. In addition, there may be employees who express concerns about complicated and cumbersome processes that delay deliveries to customers or add unnecessary cost.

Most processes can be corrected and improved by qualified employees who are focused on doing things better, even if it means making changes in processes. However, there may be occasions when the help of an outside specialist is appropriate.

CHAPTER 6

The Fourth **"P"**

"PERFORMETRICS"

The Fourth **"P"**

"PERFORMETRICS"

"WOW!" companies continuously monitor performance in a variety of areas, not all of which are financial measures. They track past, current, and future indicators that will keep them informed regarding progress toward their plan, and ultimately, their Vision. This chapter will describe Steps 19 through 23, all devoted to ways that "WOW!" companies continuously monitor their performance at every level.

Step 19: Create Individual Performance Metrics for Each Employee

One of the most common complaints I've heard from business owners is, "I wish my people were more accountable!" On the few occasions when I get a chance to talk with the rank and file employees of those companies, one of their complaints is, "I wish I was more empowered to do my job!"

While these might sound like two entirely different issues, "WOW!" companies have figured out a way to solve both complaints with the same solution. I've created my own word for this .... **"Performetrics," which is based on measuring outcomes, not activities, by empowering employees to meet or exceed the expectations that have been agreed upon by both parties.**

If each employee and supervisor could agree on a performance expectation for that employee, then leave the employee alone to figure out how to best reach that expectation, the result would be an employee who now feels "empowered," and a supervisor who is satisfied because the employee has become "accountable" by meeting the agreed-upon performance expectation.

It's no secret in life that the things which are measured are the things that get done, and that's the premise upon which "Performetrics" is based. Here's how it works, and why it comes *after* a perpetual **planning** process, purpose-driven **people**, and documented **processes**. During the perpetual planning process, the organization agrees on quantitative, time-related expectations as part of the plan. They then design a structure (organizational chart) to deliver those outcomes, populate the structure with people who can make it happen, and develop processes to support it. With all of these things in place, it's now possible to link the quantitative, qualitative, time-related expectations to each individual job. It begins by first pipelining those expectations to the top level leaders in the organization who, in turn, translate them into **clear and precise** expectations related to the employees who report to them. They continue to push those expectations to the lowest levels of the organizations so that all of them are still linked to the high level expectations outlined in the planning meeting.

In "WOW!" companies, job descriptions are continuously updated to reflect the things that need to be done in accordance with the perpetual planning process. With an updated job description in hand the challenge is how to set an individual expectation for that job which *cannot be positively or negatively impacted by what anyone else in the organization does, or fails to do.* Setting individual quantitative, qualitative, time-related expectations for each job that meets this rule is not simple, yet it is precisely the thing that "WOW!" companies have been able to implement. Done well, the business owner feels that employees are **accountable**, and employees feel they have been **empowered.** It's almost as if each employee is operating his/her own little company as a subset of the larger company.

Most organizations understand the concept of "performetrics" when applied to sales people, since sales goals and quotas are generally standard practice in the majority of companies. In "WOW!" companies, sales people also follow very well-defined *processes,* including a list of specific target accounts and regular call reports to track their activities and progress with each of those accounts. However, even in sales positions the compensation plans are often outdated or not aligned with outcomes that are under the control of the sales person. While there are certainly exceptions to this, it's normally good to have at least 30 percent of a sales person's compensation dependent upon his or her performance, and that portion of compensation should be based on activities that are within the control of the sales person, not subject to a penalty or windfall due to something outside of the sales person's control.

It is more difficult to arrive at "performetrics" for other positions in most companies, but it CAN BE and IS done by "WOW!" organizations. In order to demonstrate this process, let's use the example of Maria, whose job it is to process invoices. Based on the high level expectations outlined in the planning process, Maria's supervisor met with her to discuss and agree on her productivity expectations for the upcoming year. Specifically, Maria had averaged eight invoices per hour in the past, but her supervisor was hopeful that she would be willing to improve her productivity to ten invoices per hour next year. During their discussion, Maria said she didn't think she could agree to ten invoices per hour unless she had a new computer that was much faster. When the supervisor agreed to provide the new computer, Maria was very sure she could meet the new expectations. Her supervisor informed her that she would receive incentive compensation once she exceeded an average of ten invoices per hour each month provided that she continued to meet the existing standards for accuracy, which had not changed. It seemed that both Maria and her supervisor were happy with the agreement that they had negotiated. Maria felt empowered, and her supervisor felt like Maria was being held accountable.

At the end of the first month, Maria had fallen back into her old productivity range of eight invoices per hour. When her supervisor confronted her with the fact that she had not met the expectations upon which they had agreed, Maria legitimately responded, "I'm not able to average ten invoices per hour because the sales department has not generated enough invoices for me to meet that expectation!" The supervisor then realized that he and Maria had agreed on an expectation that was being adversely affected by someone else's failure to perform, so he and Maria sat side-by-side to figure out a solution.

After a short discussion they agreed that Maria's expectations should have been six minutes per invoice, not ten invoices per hour. Under this restated metric, if there are too few invoices to keep Maria busy, she'll be motivated to complete her invoices as quickly as possible and then approach her supervisor looking for additional work rather than sacrificing incentive compensation. This will likely compel her supervisor to put more pressure on the sales department, move Maria to another job for part of the day so he can make good use of her time, or possibly reduce the number of people processing invoices. This sort of logic is what enables "WOW!" companies to become so efficient, since over a period of time they find a variety of areas where unnecessary expenses are being incurred. In the case of Maria, if she can average less than six minutes per invoice she'll begin to receive incentive compensation for the portion that goes beyond expectations. It's important to note that Maria is not entitled to incentive compensation for simply meeting the expectation of six minutes per invoice, since that's why she receives a base hourly wage; the incentive begins to kick-in only after she exceeds the expectation and her work remains within the quality standards established (measured by percent accuracy).

Step 20: Conduct Regular Performance Appraisals

In "WOW!" companies, most "performetrics" include three standards for each employee. One is quantitative, one is qualitative, and the third is behavioral to make sure that employees don't become so focused on productivity that they cause problems in the workplace and upset the culture. Using Maria as an example, the behavioral rating can be determined by surveying employees in the departments that either feed work to Maria, or are fed work by Maria after she has completed her part of the process.

Most companies have some sort of performance appraisal process, but many lack specific quantitative expectations for each job. Ideally, performance appraisals should be conducted at least annually, and should include more than behavioral factors.

I've seen no one do this better than Alternate Solutions Healthnet, the company I referred to earlier regarding the topic of culture. David and Tessie Ganzsarto's leadership and passion drove them to relentlessly pursue their dream of becoming the best provider of service to patients AND the best place for nurses and therapists to work. To make that happen they translated their Vision and plan into a series of high-level organizational expectations that cascaded down to where they were converted to individual metrics for each employee. These are specific quantitative, qualitative, and behavioral metrics for each employee that were established each quarter and compelled employees to become more efficient while also improving the quality of patient care, two things that the industry had traditionally believed could not be done at the same time. That is, becoming more efficient was believed to be a contributor to short-cuts and poorer care, whereas Alternate Solutions' new model found exactly the opposite to be true. In their humility, neither David nor Tessie will likely make this claim, but from my perspective I find it difficult to believe that any other home health care company provides higher quality care or does it with any more efficiency.

Many organizations provide group or team standards rather than the individual metrics just described. While there is nothing wrong with arrangements that reward teams for exceeding expectations, "WOW!" companies place a much greater emphasis on individual performance. The reason is simple. Employees who are top performers often feel like they're being held back in a team or group incentive arrangement, and may be more apt to leave the organization in favor of another environment that will recognize their individual achievements.

If you'd like to implement individual "performetrics" in your organization be extremely careful not to jump into it too quickly. "WOW!" companies generally start with those who report directly to the leader so they can jointly learn more about how to choose the appropriate things to measure for each individual, and then determine reasonable expectations for the thing(s) being measured. It's not unusual to identify things that have never been measured before, so you first have to start tracking them before you can begin to decide what a reasonable expectation should be for future performance.

On the following pages you will see some sample measures to get you started, but there are many thousands of others depending upon the organization and the specific duties outlined in each job description. You'll also see a detailed explanation of how to implement "performetrics" in your organization using a three-step process called "Clear Expectations." Sample forms are also included.

Assuming you complete this exercise at the outset of each year or each quarter as part of your perpetual planning process, you will actually have up-to-date job descriptions each time you go through the "Clear Expectations" process!

Some Sample Measurements Used in "Performetrics"

Number of customer complaints (can also be measured as a percentage of sales, not just a raw number)

Number of mistakes or quality issues (can also be measured as percentage of sales or production)

Accident rate (percentage of total working hours lost due to accidents)

Brand awareness (usually measured by a survey company, and compared to results of previous survey)

Customer satisfaction index (usually measured by survey, and compared to results of previous survey)

Employee turnover (measured as percentage; note that some turnover is good and necessary)

Employee satisfaction index (usually measured by survey, and compared to results of previous survey)

Percent of employees who have some type of certification (used where tech training is essential)

Inventory turns (sales divided by inventory, which can vary widely by industry)

Percent of product delivered on-time (make sure there is clear definition of "on-time")

Percent of quotes delivered on-time (the definition of "on-time" varies by company and industry)

Forecast accuracy (especially when sales people need to help plan for sales jumps and declines)

Days sales outstanding ("DSO" is a way to measure how many days it takes to get paid)

Secret shopper score (can be retail, or can be a method to evaluate a phone operator or receptionist)

Total sales per employee (total sales divided by the number of full-time equivalent employees)

Labor utilization percentage (billable labor as a percentage of all labor cost)

Customer retention rate (percent of existing customers who are retained, not lost to competitors)

Percent of sales generated by new customers (measures ability to cold call and secure new customers)

Percent of sales generated by new products (measures new product innovation/R&D)

Invoice accuracy (percent of error-free invoices)

Order accuracy (percent of error-free orders)

Order fill rate (to reduce back-orders and promote good inventory planning)

Percent of deadlines met (especially good measure for software developers or ad agency employees)

Average days to fill open positions (good for HR people and recruiters)

Employee cooperation rating (survey of other employees who feed work to, or get work from, an employee; a measure of how well an employee "plays with others")

Example of a Blended Solution

Assume a company has a lot of scientists in a production environment where they are making a very volatile chemical. On one hand, the business owner wants them to produce a minimum quantity of x each day, and on the other hand he does not want them to sacrifice quality, since a product failure could cause major losses for customers.

Further adding to the situation is the fact that the volatile chemical can explode if the scientists try to push volume over the expected levels in order to receive a bonus.

Here's a possible solution. Each employee is awarded 5 percent of base pay for exceeding EITHER the quantity or quality expectation. If the employee exceeds BOTH the quantity and quality goals, he/she receives 15 percent (not 10 percent) of base pay. However, if there is an accident of any kind, no incentive compensation is paid for that period, even if the quantity and quality expectations have been exceeded.

Performetrics: The Three-Step "Clear Expectations" Process

Before an organization can effectively implement "performetrics," there must be a clearly articulated Vision (ideal state, or end point) for the organization, and a strategic plan designed to achieve it.

Within the strategic plan, there must be specific expectations—quantitative, qualitative, and time related. Expectations are things that can be measured, and can serve as the focal point for establishing standards of performance for everyone in the organization. That is, if the expectations are aligned with the plan, and the plan is designed to achieve the Vision, then the expectations should cascade down through the organization and be translated into specific performance expectations for every employee.

Assuming there is a clearly articulated Vision, and a realistic strategic plan (with expectations) to achieve the Vision, then the accountability model can be implemented through the three-phase process described in the pages that follow. Forms are included to assist with each step.

Steps 1(A) and 1(B) – Determining the Duties of Each Job *(See Job Analysis Form)*

For a period of at least one month, each employee should keep track of any tasks they work on for more than *5 percent* of their time, and the actual amount of time devoted to each task. The purpose of this exercise is to determine how each employee spends a typical month at work.

After the employee has calculated the results of the time-tracking described above, using the Job Analysis forms 1(A) and 1(B) included in the next pages, the employee and his or her supervisor should *separately* prepare a list of the major duties for which that employee is responsible. It is not necessary to list every item. The purpose here is to identify the key tasks that, when added together, *consume at least 80 percent of the employee's time.*

Step 2 – Getting Clarity on Expectations for Each Job *(See Form to be Completed by Employee & Supervisor)*

The employee and supervisor then meet, compare lists, and together agree on the key tasks that the employee should be performing on a regular basis using the form included in the next pages. Note that in this step the focus is on those tasks that account for *at least 10 percent of their time*, versus 5 percent in Steps 1(A) and 1(B), since the objective is to shorten the list to key tasks, not all activities. This is actually a great way to update the job description on a regular basis.

After agreeing on what the major duties are for the job, the goal is **to identify the few items on the list that are totally within the control of the job-holder**. That is, the supervisor and employee must jointly agree on which of those tasks or duties cannot be positively or negatively affected by what anyone else in the organization does, or fails to do.

Step 3 – Creating the "Performetrics" Agreement *(See Form:"Performetrics"Agreement)*

After jointly agreeing on which duties are totally within the control of the job-holder, using the "Performetrics" Agreement form, the employee and supervisor should assign **quantitative** performance standards for the upcoming year, possibly by quarter or month if appropriate. Note that these standards are **negotiated**, since the employee is agreeing that he or she will meet or exceed the standards that have been established. Standards are NOT "stretch goals." This is the "expected" level of performance. Only when performance *exceeds* the standard is it considered to be beyond expectations.

Depending upon the level of the position in the organization, there could be as few as one standard, or as many as five or six. In general, the lower the employee's position in the organization, the fewer standards there will be, since there will likely be very few duties over which the employee has total control at the lower levels. For example, a production worker might have standards for individual productivity and quality, whereas the Plant Manager might be judged on overall productivity, labor hours, overtime, quality, safety, scrap, etc.... Similarly, a telemarketer might have standards for number of outbound calls and/or number of appointments set for the field sales reps, while the Vice President of Sales might have standards for total sales, gross profit percentage, percentage of new business versus existing business, and number of sales calls.

The supervisor and subordinate each sign the document and retain a copy for regular review. Depending upon the level of the position within the organization, the employee and supervisor should review the "Performetrics" Agreement together, either monthly or quarterly. This does not require a lot of time, and it maintains focus on the things that matter.

STEP 1(A): Job Analysis Form

TO BE COMPLETED BY JOB-HOLDER

Job Title: _____

Name of Current Job-Holder: _____

Job-Holder Supervisor's Name: _____

Date: _____

Only List MAJOR Duties: (Duties that require **5% or more** of your time)

1. _____
2. _____
3. _____
4. _____
5. _____
6. _____
7. _____
8. _____
9. _____
10. _____
11. _____
12. _____
13. _____
14. _____
15. _____

Clear Expectations

STEP 1(B): Job Analysis Form

TO BE COMPLETED BY SUPERVISOR

Job Title: _____

Name of Current Job-Holder: _____

Job-Holder Supervisor's Name: _____

Date: _____

Only List MAJOR Duties: (Duties that require **5% or more** of your time)

1. _____
2. _____
3. _____
4. _____
5. _____
6. _____
7. _____
8. _____
9. _____
10. _____
11. _____
12. _____
13. _____
14. _____
15. _____

Clear Expectations

STEP 2: Job-holder and Supervisor Complete Together Using Information from Step 1(A) and Step 1(B)

Job Title: _____

Name of Current Job-Holder: _____

Job-Holder Supervisor's Name: _____

Date: _____

Only List MAJOR Duties: (Duties that require **10% or more** of your time)	**Full Authority to Act?** Yes or No
1. _____	_____
2. _____	_____
3. _____	_____
4. _____	_____
5. _____	_____
6. _____	_____
7. _____	_____
8. _____	_____
9. _____	_____
10. _____	_____

Job-Holder's Signature: _____

Supervisor's Signature: _____

Clear-Expectations

STEP 3: "Performetrics" Agreement

Job Title: _____ Name of Current Job-Holder: _____

Time Period Covered: _____ Date: _____ Name of Supervisor: _____

			These Columns for Future Use	
Duties for Which Job-Holder Has Total Authority to Act	**Method of Measurement**	**Expected Outcome**	**Actual Outcome**	**% Over (+) or Under (-)**
1. _____	_____	_____	_____	_____
2. _____	_____	_____	_____	_____
3. _____	_____	_____	_____	_____
4. _____	_____	_____	_____	_____

We agree on the duties for which the Job-Holder has total authority, the method of measurement, and the expected outcomes above:

Job-Holder Signature: _____ Supervisor Signature: _____

Date: _____ Date: _____

Clear-Expectations

Step 21: Conduct Employee Surveys

"WOW!" organizations monitor their culture with periodic surveys of their employees. The frequency of these surveys depends on how rapidly the organization is changing. In most organizations it's good to survey the employees every two years, but when things are changing quickly, annual surveys may be more appropriate.

The key thing to remember about surveys is that employee expectations are often raised when they are asked to give their candid opinions, so be prepared to act on the results. In addition, even in the most comfortable cultures, employees are often apprehensive about expressing their true opinions, so take the necessary steps to make employees feel confident that their responses will be confidential. To ease their apprehensions, you can hire an outside firm to conduct the survey, or use an online service to anonymously capture responses. Some business owners set-up a computer in the breakroom and allow each employee to enter their responses online during company time, which also increases the percentage of employees who participate.

Although business owners might think online surveys will make employees feel comfortable that their responses will remain confidential, some of them will still fear their replies can somehow be traced to them. In those situations, it may be appropriate to offer employees the option of using a preprinted survey form that can be taken home. The form can be completed by a friend or family member so that the employee's handwriting can't be recognized, and can then be mailed to the employer in a pre-addressed postage-paid envelope. While the latter may seem extreme, it's surprising how many employees are fearful of expressing their true opinions unless they are absolutely certain that no one will be able to trace their responses back to them. So remember to take whatever steps you think are necessary to get candid and honest feedback.

The following pages include a sample survey that you may find helpful. I've used the term "Under-Current" to describe it, since calmness on top of the water can often hide turmoil beneath. The sample survey enables the answers to be quantified so that the business owner can actually track how scores have changed with each successive use of the survey, and it also allows space for employees to record their comments.

"Under-Current" Employee Satisfaction Survey

Using the rating system below, please rate the degree to which you agree with each statement by entering your rating on the line next to that statement. Please feel free to add any comments in the space below each statement.

Rating System:

NA = Does not apply/don't know
0 = Strongly disagree/No evidence to support this statement
1 = Somewhat disagree
2 = Undecided
3 = Somewhat agree
4 = Strongly agree

Your Rating

Vision and Mission

_____ I have a clear understanding of where the organization is going

Comments: _____

_____ I understand how my work directly affects where the organization is going

Comments: _____

Values and Beliefs

_____ The organization's values and beliefs are clearly stated and communicated to all employees

Comments: _____

_____ The values and beliefs are consistently demonstrated throughout the organization

Comments: _____

Strategy

_____ The organization has a strategic plan

Comments: _____

_____ The strategic plan is communicated to the entire organization

Comments: _____

Customer Focus

____ The organization has clearly defined the types of customers they want to serve

Comments: _____

____ The organization is extremely focused on the needs of customers

Comments: _____

Expectations

____ The organization has clearly identified how my success is measured

Comments: _____

____ The organization provides me with regular feedback regarding how well I am meeting expectations

Comments: _____

Time

____ Timeliness of serving customers is a top priority of our organization

Comments: _____

____ I have specific and measurable standards I must meet that are related to timeliness of response

Comments: _____

Quality

____ Quality of the product/service we provide is a top priority of our organization

Comments: _____

____ I have specific and measurable standards I must meet that are related to the quality of my work

Comments: _____

Cost

___ Our organization is constantly focused on reducing the cost to make or provide our product/service

Comments: _____

___ I have specific and measurable standards I must meet that are related to the cost of what I do

Comments: _____

Customer Satisfaction

___ Our organization is focused on measuring customer satisfaction on a regular basis

Comments: _____

___ I have specific and measurable standards I must meet that are related to customer satisfaction

Comments: _____

The Workplace Facilities

___ The physical environment where I work is safe

Comments: _____

___ The physical environment where I work is healthy for me

Comments: _____

Culture

___ Honesty is a highly-valued and non-negotiable trait of every employee in our organization

Comments: _____

___ I am treated fairly

Comments: _____

Communications

___ The organization does a good job of sharing information with employees

Comments: _____

___ I am comfortable sharing my ideas and opinions with my manager or supervisor

Comments: _____

Tools and Information

___ I have the information that I need to do my job well

Comments: _____

___ I have the tools and equipment I need to do my job well

Comments: _____

Respect

___ Employees throughout the organization treat one another with dignity and respect at all times

Comments: _____

___ The organization recognizes the need for balance between work life and personal life

Comments: _____

Opportunity for Growth

___ There are opportunities for me to advance within this organization when I'm ready

Comments: _____

___ The company provides me with the necessary training and development to grow professionally

Comments: _____

Compensation and Benefits

___ I am fairly compensated for the work I do

Comments: _____

___ My employee benefits are comparable to those offered by other organizations

Comments: _____

Company Leadership

___ The leader of our organization has strong leadership skills

Comments: _____

___ The leader of our organization treats everyone fairly and equally

Comments: _____

___ The leader of our organization is a strong communicator

Comments: _____

___ The leader of our organization acts with integrity and honesty in all dealings

Comments: _____

___ The leader of our organization has great energy and passion for what we do

Comments: _____

___ The leader of our organization is flexible

Comments: _____

___ The leader of our organization has strong listening skills

Comments: _____

___ The leader of our organization is willing to delegate

Comments: _____

Overall Satisfaction

___ I am not only happy, but also proud, to be an employee of this organization

Comments: _____

___ If one of my friends was looking for a job, I would definitely recommend working for our company

Comments: _____

Step 22: Create Tracking Reports to Maintain Control

A strategic planning process must include budgets, forecasts, cash flow projections, dashboards, and other financial reports to monitor actual performance against the plan so that quick actions can be taken when appropriate.

While most business owners recognize the value of such reports, many lack a strategic plan against which to measure performance, don't have budgets, or don't have a good handle on future cash flow.

Even if a company has a dashboard showing key performance metrics, too many of those dashboards are focused only on looking backward. That is, sometimes the business owner knows exactly what happened right up to the close of yesterday's business, but there are no components of the dashboard that provide any look into the future, like backlog of business, number of leads, requests for quotation, or other forward-looking indicators of what might be in store for the business in the next few months.

"WOW!" companies are typically extremely efficient. They have such good plans, people, processes, and performance metrics that their productivity per employee is significantly above their competitors. Although there are many more sophisticated ways to measure efficiency, one of the most popular ratios is "Total Annual Sales per Full-Time Equivalent Employee" ("Sales per FTE"). For example, if a manufacturing company has annual sales volume of $12 million, and employs 100 full-time equivalent employees, the ratio would be $120,000 per employee. Note that the term "full-time equivalent employees" refers to the number of full-time employees, plus the number of part-time employees, converted to more accurately describe how many there would actually be if they were full-time. That is, 80 full-time plus 40 half-time would translate to 100 full-time equivalent employees.

As companies move closer and closer to "WOW!" status, the ratio gets better and better and, typically, profitability also improves steadily.

It's possible to compare the efficiencies of companies in the same industry by reviewing the Total Sales per Full-Time Equivalent ratio from one company to the next. In the example above, it may be a matter of first determining the company's SIC or NAICS Code, and then asking your commercial banker to compare your company's ratio to others with the same SIC Code or NAICS Code, since many banks have access to those statistics and use them regularly to evaluate the financial strength and efficiency of their business clients. For "WOW!" companies this ratio often reaches levels that most in their industry don't think possible.

Step 23: Monitor Board Performance

As mentioned in Step 12, not only is it important that you determine what skill sets you need in employees, but you should also decide what type of expertise is required from each board member in order to implement the plan, whether it's marketing, finance, operations, or some other area of focus.

In Step 23, the objective is to evaluate the performance of the board to assess how well they are meeting your expectations, both individually and collectively, in the same way that you evaluate the performance of employees. Here are some questions you should ask yourself:

- Are you getting what you want from the meetings?

- Is each member contributing?

- Are they fulfilling the expectations you established for them when you invited them to become board members?

- Is it time to replace any of them?

- Is it time to review the term limits of each member to determine if/when a replacement should be made?

Keep in mind that you should also be asking your board members to evaluate you, including your preparation for meetings, the information you're providing them, how well you run the board meetings, your willingness to listen, and how qualified they think you are to move the company forward.

WOW!

CHAPTER 7

The Fifth **"P"**

PASSION to Be the Best

The Fifth **"P"**

PASSION to Be the Best

We have already established that many "WOW!" companies have passionate leaders! While defining "passionate" can be difficult in the context of business leaders, most of us immediately recognize passionate leaders when we see them. The leaders of many "WOW!" companies I've encountered have that passion "oozing out of them" for the lack of a better description. It's the same type of passion most of us have probably observed in a teacher or professor who truly and genuinely loves a particular subject. We often meet people in our everyday lives who have given up fame and fortune to pursue their passion. This is the same sort of behavior demonstrated by passionate business owners.

There are certainly many talented, dedicated leaders who aren't necessarily passionate but have advanced their organizations to great levels, including some in the "WOW!" status. From my perspective, these executives are truly "professional managers" who could take their talent to other companies with similar success, and they are major contributors to the job growth and prosperity of our private enterprise system. However, adding a little passion to those leaders seems to do two things—it gets their organizations to "WOW!" status **faster, and makes it more likely that they'll remain there.**

The passion of the leader has absolutely nothing to do with education or experience. Passionate leaders tend to be humble, yet confident. They are typically calm, yet assertive. They are genuinely interested in providing the very best product or service to their customers, and creating a work environment that allows each employee to reach his or her full potential, even if it means the employee might eventually leave the company to pursue his or her own dream. They proactively invest in their people, and in becoming the very best provider to their customers.

- **Some of them are passionate about** *what the business does*
- **Some are passionate about being** *the best, regardless of what the business does*
- **Some are passionate about** *both*!

What I'm about to say is not meant to be a statement of religion or philosophy, but it is important to realize that many passionate leaders subscribe to the idea of servant leadership, and actually view their business as a means to minister to others, either directly or indirectly.

Because of their humility and drive to have the very best organization possible, passionate leaders recognize their own shortcomings and surround themselves with talented people who can offer the expertise they need. They do this by bringing employees into the organization who are more skilled than they are in specific functions of the business. In addition, they have an Outside Board that they rely on heavily for on-going, high-level advice regarding the future of the business, as well as personal advisors who can bring the guidance they need in areas like personal finance, banking, law, insurance, health, etc….

A Word About Outside Boards

Passionate leaders are not only willing, but *anxious*, to seek regular and on-going input from experts who are smarter than they are in specific areas of business, so they don't hesitate to form an Outside Board. Remember that you don't have to be a passionate leader to have a strong Outside Board; indeed, most well-run companies have one.

A "WOW!" company is never too large or too small to seek the advice of qualified, **objective** outsiders. These are people who have already successfully navigated the entrepreneurial pasture, and have probably gotten their shoes dirty a few times.

"WOW!" companies put together Outside Boards with a specific meeting schedule, typically quarterly. Meetings can involve a few hours, or a full day. There is an agenda for each meeting, and the members sometimes help to identify topics they believe are key issues.

For companies with fewer than 200 employees, a group of three unbiased outsiders is usually adequate. They should be from different disciplines, like finance, marketing, or operations, and they should also be experts in their fields. They'll bring the kind of talent that most businesses probably can't afford on a day-to-day basis. Their focus should be primarily on the more strategic type issues, but they may occasionally get involved in other areas as well. By no means should they get into the minute details of the business, but they can certainly provide some basic guidance in those areas.

Some "WOW!" companies prefer Boards of Directors, while others choose Boards of Advisors. There is a legal difference, so you should consult your attorney before you decide how you want to structure the board. While it's certainly acceptable to have an attorney, accountant, etc., on the board, do NOT allow it to be *your* attorney, accountant, or other paid advisor, since you're already paying them for their advice, and there's always a chance that they might not be as objective as those who have nothing to gain or lose by providing advice. Board members absolutely MUST be independent thinkers!

Before deciding what types of people are needed, "WOW!" companies take a candid look at their organizations to determine their greatest weaknesses and strategic opportunities. They then identify potential board candidates who can help them overcome those weaknesses and take advantage of the opportunities.

"WOW!" companies establish term limits from the very start, and stagger them so that only one member leaves, and is replaced, at a time. Typical terms are one, two, or three years, and they provide the business owner and board member with the opportunity to discontinue the relationship or, if appropriate, extend the engagement for another term, usually one additional year at a time. In the majority of cases, either the business owner or board member will conclude that it's time to end the engagement after four or five years, since by then the board member has typically imparted the majority of his or her expertise. In addition, after a few years it's likely that the needs of the business have changed. For example, the company may have been weak in marketing when the board was initially formed, but three years later a strong full-time marketing person joined the company and, therefore, there was no longer a need for that type of expertise on the board.

The question regarding the potential liability of a board member, or how to limit or protect board members from possible liability, is one that should be directed to an attorney who is well-versed in boards. Some business owners provide board members with a letter of indemnification so they are personally indemnified in the event that the board is named in a legal proceeding. Others provide Directors and Officers insurance, although it can be expensive. Regardless of whether a company chooses a Board of Directors or Board of Advisors, it is essential that both the business owner and board members are aware of possible liability, and take the necessary steps to mitigate such issues.

It is also common practice to ask each board member to sign a confidentiality agreement since proprietary information will be disclosed by the company. Here again, it is very important to seek competent legal guidance regarding how to protect confidentiality, since board members will be exposed to sensitive and proprietary information during the time they serve.

While some board members do not expect to be paid, it is a good idea to offer them compensation commensurate with their experience level. In lieu of compensation, some might prefer that a donation be made to a charity in their name. Others will serve on your board simply because they enjoy it. If the first question they ask is how much they'll be compensated, then it's time to consider another candidate.

Board members can come from a variety of sources. Your company's attorney or accounting firm can often provide the names of some candidates.

When meeting to interview the potential board candidate for the first time, it's good to have a booklet that includes company history, organization chart, a description of what the company does, products/services, the markets/customers served, some basic financial numbers (but nothing proprietary during the interview), and what is expected from each board member.

After finding the first board member, the business owner and first member should choose the next member *jointly* to reduce the chance of future personality conflicts between members, and so on with the next member.

The "P.I.E." Phenomenon

It's important to note that having a passionate leader at the helm creates some potential future risks for the organization. When the passionate leader is no longer in charge for whatever reason, there is rarely a successor who possesses the same level of passion.

Although *there are definitely exceptions,* over a period of time, each successive leader generally demonstrates a little less passion, not through any personal shortcoming, but simply because the subsequent leaders are likely to be more passionate about something else besides the business. They definitely have a keen *interest* in the business, but it's generally not passion.

It's certainly possible to stay in the "WOW!" category with a leader who is *interested*. However, there can be times when the leadership of an organization regresses to a level below *interested*. It occasionally occurs in multi-generational family-owned businesses when leadership has moved from the *passion* of the founder, to the *interest* of his or her children and grandchildren, to a later generation whose approach can best be described as *entitled*. This is something I call the **"Passionate – Interested – Entitled" (P.I.E.) Phenomenon**. If allowed to run its course, it can be a contributor to the disappearance of a family business that may have operated successfully for more than one hundred years. This is not to say that subsequent generations of the family weren't passionate about something. Indeed, many of them may have become passionate about charitable activities or other noble causes, but somehow the business didn't receive the necessary attention.

For those truly well-managed companies that do NOT have passionate leaders at the top, here are a few observations that may be of help going forward.

First, a leader should never stop trying to stay qualified for the job as it changes. In the same way that others in the organization need to grow and develop to remain qualified for their jobs, the leader must do so as well. In some cases it may even be appropriate for the leader to relinquish the leadership position to someone more qualified, but only after there is clear evidence that the leader has reached full potential.

Second, if an organization continuously and candidly re-evaluates itself and finds it is unable to move beyond the "Ouch," "Ho-Hum," or "Gee-Whiz" category, then the constraint is likely related to the limited capacity of the leader to lead. For example, over a period of years, perhaps the leader is able to move the organization from "Ouch" to "Ho-Hum," and maybe even temporarily "top-out" in the "Gee-Whiz" category for a brief time before falling back into "Ho-Hum." In that case the leadership potential has probably been reached, and has now become the constraint on further advancement for the company toward the "WOW!" classification of professional management.

Remember this about passionate leadership. Strong leaders can definitely get organizations into the "WOW!" category, even if that leader might not be described as passionate. However, **passion seems to play a major role in how quickly a leader can take an organization into the "WOW!" category, and how likely it is that the organization will remain there**.

CHAPTER 8

Is My Business "Ouch," "Ho-Hum," "Gee-Whiz," or **"WOW!"**?

Is My Business "Ouch," "Ho-Hum," "Gee-Whiz," or **"WOW!"**?

We've spent a lot of time talking about how to become a "WOW!" business, so it may be helpful to determine what stage your business is in right now, and specifically identify what needs to be done to move it toward "WOW!" status.

Here are 84 questions that can be used to determine the current status of your business. The questions are arranged into four categories that correspond to the first four "P's," while the fifth "P" ("Passion") manifests itself in how quickly your company can advance, and how long it can remain in the "WOW!" category. The answer to each question can only be "yes," or "no"—that is, there can be no "maybe" answers. If the answer is not 100 percent "yes," then it's a "no." You'll note 16 of the questions are worth two points, so that the total possible score is 100 points. At the end of the survey you will be instructed on how to calculate your score, which will then indicate whether your business is categorized as "Ouch," "Ho-Hum," "Gee-Whiz," or "WOW!"

Current Status Survey

The First "P" – PLANNING as a Perpetual Process *(See Chapter Three)*

_____ 1. Do you have an up-to-date Personal Vision?

_____ 2. Do you have a Vision for your organization that is regularly reviewed to determine if it still reflects what you want the organization to become someday?

_____ 3. Is your organizational Vision clearly understood by every employee?

_____ 4. Can every employee explain your organizational Vision without assistance?

_____ 5. Does every employee understand how the organizational Vision relates to his/her job?

_____ 6. Is your organizational Vision measurable so that you can tell if/when it is achieved?

_____ 7. Do you have a Mission for your organization?

_____ 8. Is your Mission clearly understood by every employee?

_____ 9. Can every employee explain your organization's Mission without assistance?

_____10. Do you have Values and Beliefs that are accurate and up to date?

_____11. Are your Values and Beliefs in writing so that all employees are exposed to them regularly?

_____12. Are your Values and Beliefs consistently demonstrated by everyone in your organization?

_____13. Do you have a strategic plan that covers a three or five-year period and is updated at least once each year?

_____14. At least annually, do you analyze each market segment to determine key factors like competition, government regulations, changes in technology, demographics, industry trends, etc...?

_____15. At least annually, do you analyze your strengths, weaknesses, opportunities, and threats in each market segment?

_____16. Within each market segment, do you know the strengths and weaknesses of each major competitor, and how they compare to yours?

_____17. Do you feel comfortable that you know who your major competitors will be three years from now?

_____18. At least annually, do you evaluate your market segments based on Ideal Attributes so that each segment can be "scored" and ranked? **2 PTS**

_____19. Are you gaining market share in each market segment?

_____20. At least annually, do you evaluate your customers based on Ideal Attributes so that each customer can be "scored" and ranked? **2 PTS**

_____21. At least annually, do you dig deeply enough to identify whether or not you have a true "core competency?"

_____22. At least annually, do you take a fresh look at identifying no more than three key issues that need to be addressed, regardless of whether those issues are short-term/operational, or longer-term/strategic? **2 PTS**

_____23. Do you set quantitative and time-phased expectations/outcomes for each key issue that will enable you to determine when that issue has been successfully addressed? **2 PTS**

_____24. Do you create action items to address each key issue, assign specific people to each action item, and establish firm due dates for their completion?

_____25. Do you allocate the resources necessary to implement the plan?

_____26. Do you hold regularly scheduled meetings to review action items and due dates, and hold people responsible for attending all of those meetings and reporting progress on each item assigned to them? **2 PTS**

The Second "P" – PEOPLE Who "Fit," Today and Tomorrow *(See Chapter Four)*

_____27. Do you have an organizational chart that is up-to-date?

_____28. Is your organizational chart aligned in a manner that will enable your strategy to be implemented?

_____29. Are the reporting lines on your organizational chart absolutely clear to everyone?

_____30. Do you have a succession plan for every position, including your own?

_____31. Are there up-to-date job descriptions for every position in your organization?

_____32. Do you know specifically what skill sets are needed in each position on your organizational chart?

_____33. Do you objectively evaluate the degree to which each person meets the required skill sets in each position?

_____34. Are you willing to hire others who have greater skill sets than you in order to achieve your organization's Vision? **2 PTS**

_____35. Do you have an independent Outside Board that does not include friends, family, your accountant, your attorney, your banker, or others whose advice you are already paying to get? **2 PTS**

_____36. Do the skill sets of your board members match the skill sets you need to help you implement your strategic plan? **2 PTS**

_____37. Do you replace board members periodically so that your board possesses the skill sets you need as your strategic plan changes? **2 PTS**

_____38. Are you willing to listen to, and act on, suggestions from outside advisors who have expertise in areas you don't? **2 PTS**

_____39. Do you have job classifications that show the relative rankings for every position in the organization?

_____40. Do you have compensation ranges established for every job classification?

_____41. Is at least 30 percent of your typical sales person's compensation based on performance incentives?

_____42. Do you have an incentive component for compensation in every position, not just sales?

_____43. Does the person in charge of the organization truly possess the skill sets necessary to effectively lead the organization for at least another year? **2 PTS**

_____44. Does every manager reporting to the leader have the skill sets necessary to take the organization where it needs to go for at least another year? **2 PTS**

_____45. Does every person at every level in your current organization have the skill sets required to perform his or her current job?

_____46. Do you have an established budget specifically designated for the development of your employees?

_____47. Do you and your organization proactively develop each employee to his or her full potential?

_____48. Do you have a documented and effective process for recruiting the talent that your organization needs in order to achieve your strategic plan?

_____49. Do you utilize some sort of pre-employment testing or assessment tool to help predict how well a prospective employee will "fit" your culture?

_____50. Do you generally hire slowly, rather than rushing to find people to fill vacant positions?

_____51. Has every one of your strong employees remained with your company over the past year?

_____52. Do you have a consistent process for handling employees whose skill sets are limited, and need to be re-assigned or separated from your organization?

_____53. Do you develop a plan for personal development so that each employee knows exactly what they need to do in order to stay qualified for their current position?

_____54. Do you take a positive and proactive approach to managing your culture?

_____55. Do you have an up-to-date employee manual?

_____56. Is your employee manual written in a positive tone?

_____57. Do you consistently and quickly dismiss employees who are poor performers or don't fit your culture, even if they are related to you?

_____58. Do you take a positive and respectful approach when weeding out employees who don't fit?

The Third "P" – PROCESSES *(See Chapter Five)*

_____59. Are all of your processes aligned with your strategic plan?

_____60. Are all of your processes well-documented?

_____61. Are all of your processes clear?

_____62. Are all of your processes repeatable?

_____63. Are all of your processes strictly followed?

_____64. Are all of your processes linked to job descriptions?

_____65. Do you have incentive compensation plans linked to your processes?

_____66. Are training and development built around your processes?

_____67. Are your processes continuously re-evaluated for appropriateness?

_____68. Is there someone in your organization responsible for maintaining and improving processes? **2 PTS**

_____69. Is the quality of your product or service at least on par with your strongest competitor, as measured by customer feedback (often a reflection on how well your processes are working)?

_____70. Is the technology of your product or service at least on par with your strongest competitor, as measured by customer feedback (often a reflection on how well your processes are working)?

_____71. Are you delivering your products or services at least as quickly as your strongest competitor (often a reflection on how well your processes are working)?

The Fourth "P" –"PERFORMETRICS" *(See Chapter Six)*

_____72. Do you set individual performance metrics for each employee at the beginning of each year or each quarter? **2 PTS**

_____73. Do you conduct performance appraisals with each employee at least annually?

_____74. Do you conduct a survey of employees at least every two years to monitor your culture and the level of satisfaction among your employees?

_____75. Do you report the results of your employee survey to those who participated?

_____76. Do you take actions stemming from information obtained through employee surveys?

_____77. Are all budgets and forecasts tied to, and in alignment with, your strategic plan?

_____78. Within 15 percent accuracy, can you forecast the amount of cash you will have on hand sixty days from now? **2 PTS**

_____79. Can you accurately assess your financial performance by product, service, market, and customer?

_____80. Do you manage the business by a few key metrics that you review at least weekly?

_____81. Do you have key metrics that provide you with an indication of what your business will look like at least ninety days from now, rather than being focused only on what happened in the past?

_____82. If you divide your total annual sales by the number of full-time equivalent employees you have, does that number exceed the average for your industry?

_____83. In reviewing the ratio from the question above, is that ratio improving each year, indicating that you are becoming more and more efficient? **2 PTS**

_____84. Can you say with certainty that all incentive compensation plans/bonuses are based on formulas, not discretion?

Scoring

As stated at the outset, there are 84 questions, but the maximum possible score is 100 points, since 16 of the questions are weighted two points and the other 68 are each weighted one point. If your total score is 90 or higher for "yes" responses, you're in the "WOW!" category. The scores for the other three categories can have some overlap between them based on which questions had "no" for answers. However, in general a score of less than 35 would categorize an organization in the "Ouch" stage, 35 to 69 would be "Ho-Hum," and 70 to 89 would be "Gee-Whiz." Do NOT get hung-up on whether your organization is a "high-end Ouch" or a "low-end Ho-Hum." Instead, focus your attention on the _reasons_ why you scored the way you did!

Regardless of the score, the key is to continue moving up the scale by viewing this journey as a repetitive cycle as described in the next chapter, "The Perfect Path." Remember to never get complacent as you advance, since factors in the marketplace are regularly changing which can cause a reduction in any organization's score.

Passionate people can often make the journey much shorter by accelerating the rate of progress along the path, and they may be less likely to allow a score to fall due to their focus on being the best.

What Are the Next Steps?

After completing the survey above, the temptation is to immediately start doing whatever necessary to move the "no" answers to "yes," one-by-one. While that's certainly one way to approach your quest for "WOW!," you'll find that it is much more effective and will take less time if you view the process in a logical sequence, which is depicted for you graphically in the next chapter.

CHAPTER 9

The Perfect Path to
"WOW!"

The Perfect Path to
"WOW!"

Many well-run businesses have not reached the "WOW!" category, and there is absolutely nothing wrong if a business owner says, "I'm very happy with my business life, and my personal life, just the way they are." Becoming a "WOW!" business is a major commitment that requires a lot of work, and it's just not necessary to go there.

However, every business should be continuously monitoring the changes that are taking place in the world around them. These changes can catch you by surprise if you get too complacent. Even if an organization is built on the notion of continuous improvement, it can sometimes get into trouble by getting better and better at something that the market has decided it no longer needs. It's far better to continuously monitor the marketplace before determining exactly what needs to be continuously improved!

Because of the changing business environment, the first four "P's" outlined in this book must be viewed as a recurring cycle so that every time the business owner feels that those first four "P's" have been successfully addressed, he or she immediately realizes that it's time to repeat the cycle. With each new cycle, the business comes closer and closer to "WOW!" status.

The Continuous Cycle

Below is a step-by-step, logical sequence that many business owners have found to be helpful. The first four "P's" are included in these twenty-three steps. The fifth "P," passion to be the best, is manifested in how quickly the company moves to "WOW!" (speed), and how likely the organization is to remain in the "WOW!" category:

Planning (Steps 1 through 10)

1. Create a Personal Vision.
2. Create an Organizational Vision, Mission, and Values (and make sure there is alignment with Personal Vision).
3. Analyze the external business environment (markets, competition, economy, technology, etc…), and be sure to do this for each market segment you serve.
4. Analyze the organization's strengths, weaknesses, opportunities, and threats (SWOT'S), and be sure to do this for each market segment you serve.
5. Review the Organizational Vision to make sure it's still realistic in view of the external business environment and SWOT's.

6. Identify/re-identify Key Issues (hopefully no more than three).

7. Establish three-year quantitative outcomes/expectations for each Key Issue (that is, "What will have happened, and by when, to let us know we have successfully addressed each issue?").

8. Create action plans with due dates, and assign each action item to a specific person.

9. Allocate the necessary resources (budgets and forecasts) to make sure the plan can be successfully implemented.

10. Establish, and strictly adhere to, a regular review process to make sure action plans and due dates are achieved.

People *(Steps 11 through 17)*

11. Determine the organizational structure (chart) required to most effectively implement the plan, and change the structure if necessary.

12. Identify the skill sets needed in each position (box) shown on the organizational chart, including the expertise you need on your Outside Board.

13. Update, or create, job descriptions for each position on the organizational chart.

14. Conduct a candid assessment of current employees to determine who immediately fits in

the new organizational chart, who can be developed to fit, and whose skills will not be adequate.

15. Establish a specific budget each year for the training and development of employees, and make a deliberate effort to spend those funds on employees.

16. Create individual development plans for existing employees who have the capability to improve their skill sets and become qualified for new positions in the organizational chart.

17. Identify what skill sets must come from new employees, and create a recruitment plan to find those needed skill sets, including established pay ranges for each position and an employee manual that clearly describes the operating environment using "positive" language.

Processes *(Step 18)*

18. Continuously evaluate and re-evaluate all processes to make certain that they are efficiently and effectively meeting the needs of customers and the organization.

Performetrics *(Steps 19 through 23)*

19. Establish individual performance metrics ("performetrics") for each employee that are tied to

the qualitative and quantitative, time-related outcomes/expectations that are outlined in the strategic plan.

20. Conduct regular performance appraisals to assess how well each employee has met the expectations outlined in the job description and individual "performetrics."

21. Conduct a periodic survey of employees to monitor the organization's culture and employee satisfaction.

22. Create the appropriate reports to track all aspects of the organization's performance compared to the outcomes and expectations outlined in the strategic plan, and continue to monitor performance against those expectations so that swift action can be taken if/when appropriate.

23. After the creation of an Outside Board possessing the skill sets defined in step number 12, continue to monitor the effectiveness of that Board, and make the necessary changes in membership to assure that the expertise on the board is appropriate for the future direction outlined in the plan.

AFTER STEP 23, REPEAT THE CYCLE, BEGINNING WITH THE PERSONAL VISION, AND CONTINUE TO

REASSESS, REVISE, AND REPEAT THE CYCLE TO MOVE CLOSER AND CLOSER TO "WOW!" STATUS.

The logical sequence and steps described above are part of a continuous cycle, as shown on page 167. It's much like a racetrack. Each time you complete a lap you return to the first step, begin the process again, and then re-evaluate your progress periodically by going through the 84 questions in Chapter Eight. Your score should be improving with each lap. The good news is that many of the 23 steps go quickly if nothing has changed since the last time you went through the cycle, so each step may, or may not, be time-consuming.

Just Follow the Path!

I wish you the very best on your quest to "WOW!" status. For those of you whose businesses have already achieved it, congratulations, since you are in rarefied air!

The purpose of this book is to define the steps, and to help you successfully progress along the path to "WOW!," or to assist you in remaining there if you've already made it. Hopefully the examples, forms, and surveys in this book will provide you with the tools you need to move forward on your own. ◯

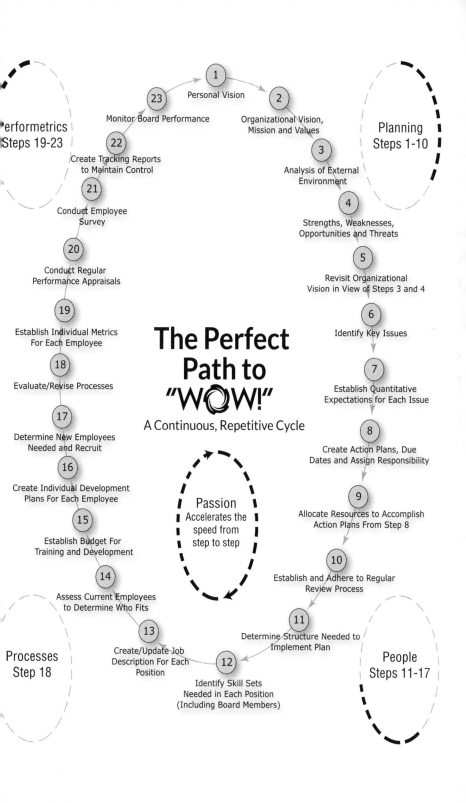

The Perfect
Path to
"WOW!"

A Continuous, Repetitive Cycle

1. Personal Vision
2. Organizational Vision, Mission and Values
3. Analysis of External Environment
4. Strengths, Weaknesses, Opportunities and Threats
5. Revisit Organizational Vision in View of Steps 3 and 4
6. Identify Key Issues
7. Establish Quantitative Expectations for Each Issue
8. Create Action Plans, Due Dates and Assign Responsibility
9. Allocate Resources to Accomplish Action Plans From Step 8
10. Establish and Adhere to Regular Review Process
11. Determine Structure Needed to Implement Plan
12. Identify Skill Sets Needed in Each Position (Including Board Members)
13. Create/Update Job Description For Each Position
14. Assess Current Employees to Determine Who Fits
15. Establish Budget For Training and Development
16. Create Individual Development Plans For Each Employee
17. Determine New Employees Needed and Recruit
18. Evaluate/Revise Processes
19. Establish Individual Metrics For Each Employee
20. Conduct Regular Performance Appraisals
21. Conduct Employee Survey
22. Create Tracking Reports to Maintain Control
23. Monitor Board Performance

Planning
Steps 1-10

People
Steps 11-17

Processes
Step 18

Performetrics
Steps 19-23

Passion
Accelerates the speed from step to step

About the Author

After spending a few years as a teacher and football coach, Bill Matthews completed graduate school and entered the business world where he gained a wide range of experience, including stints as an executive and corporate officer for a Fortune 500 company, and president of a privately-held regional financial services business.

After the company was purchased by a publicly-traded corporation, he focused his attention on his passion, advising the owners of privately-held businesses. In 1996, Bill helped create The Center for Entrepreneurial Education, now known as Aileron, a not-for-profit organization that has provided educational and advisory services to thousands of companies from its campus near Dayton, Ohio.

Spanning three decades, Bill has worked closely with business leaders to assist them with professional management, strategic planning, and the establishment of outside boards, and has served on many boards himself. He has also authored numerous articles, and two other books, *Don't Step in the Entremanure,* and *Seven T's to a Lasting Legacy.*

Through licensing arrangements, many of the best practices described in Bill's books, and in the associated toolkits, are now being used in publications and programs offered through Sandler Training in hundreds of locations worldwide.

For more information, or questions regarding information contained in this book, or in any of his other publications, go to:

WWW.GOWOWADVISORS.COM

Other Books by
BILL MATTHEWS

FIVE P'S TO A WOW BUSINESS

DON'T STEP IN THE ENTREMANURE

SEVEN T'S TO A LASTING LEGACY

FOR FREE RESOURCES AND MORE INFORMATION
ABOUT BILL MATHEWS AND THE WOW BUSINESS
ADVISORY GROUP GO TO

WWW.GOWOWADVISORS.COM

To learn more about the
WOW BUSINESS ADVISORY
E L E A R N I N G   C O U R S E
Visit below...

KNOWLEDGELINKTV.COM/SOUNDWISDOM/COURSES/THE-WOW-BUSINESS-ADVISORY

Created for entrepreneurs, business owners, and managers, the WOW! Business Advisory will help you take your organization to WOW! success by providing detailed instruction in the Five P System of Professional Management, a system currently being used by some of the world's largest corporate training companies.

Create, revise, and communicate your organizational vision, mission, beliefs, and values

Recruit, hire, and retain first-class talent

Empower your employees and enhance accountability

Included in this course:
Business Assessment
Workbook and Leader's Guide
18 Interactive Video Sessions
Tools, Exercises, Forms, Examples
And much more!